The Unofficial

Tiktok

COOKBOOK

2025

120 Viral Recipes for Snacks, Drinks, Desserts, and Kitchen Hacks!

Courtney Haney

Welcome to The Unofficial TikTok Cookbook 2025!

TikTok has transformed the way we cook, eat, and share recipes. From viral pasta dishes to creative desserts, this platform has inspired millions to try exciting new flavors and techniques. Whether you're a seasoned home chef or just starting your culinary journey, this cookbook brings you the best trending recipes, reimagined for your kitchen.

Inside, you'll find step-by-step instructions, pro tips, and variations to make each dish your own. So, grab your ingredients, hit record (if you want to share your masterpiece), and let's bring the magic of TikTok food trends to life!

Happy cooking!
Courtney Haney

TABLE OF CONTENTS

INTRODUCTION

Welcome to the Viral Kitchen

TikTok has done for cooking what it once did for dancing: turned it into a global phenomenon. Kitchens are no longer just places to follow age-old recipes handed down through generations; they're now stages for creativity, experiments, and jaw-dropping dishes that can go viral in a matter of hours. This is the essence of the Viral Kitchen, a world where simplicity meets ingenuity, and every ingredient has the potential to spark joy and a million likes.

Whether you're a seasoned chef or a complete beginner, TikTok has made cooking approachable and fun. In this cookbook, we'll dive deep into the TikTok-inspired recipes and trends that have captured the hearts (and stomachs) of millions worldwide. But first, let's explore how TikTok has transformed the culinary landscape and the tools and ingredients you'll need to get started.

How TikTok Changed Cooking

TikTok has revolutionized cooking in ways few could have imagined. With its short, engaging videos and an endless stream of creative content, TikTok has democratized the kitchen. No longer do you need to be a professional chef or have expensive equipment to make something extraordinary. Instead, the platform's bite-sized tutorials and hacks have empowered home cooks everywhere to take part in the culinary conversation.

Here are some key ways TikTok has transformed the way we cook:

- **Accessible Creativity:** TikTok has shown that anyone can cook. From students in tiny dorm kitchens to busy parents juggling mealtimes, TikTok makes cooking feel less intimidating. Complex recipes are broken down into easy, digestible steps that anyone can follow.
- **Viral Trends:** Who could have predicted that baked feta pasta or whipped coffee would become household staples overnight? TikTok's viral trends often feature recipes that are not only delicious but also photogenic, encouraging users to try them out and share their own versions.
- **Community Building:** The platform has cultivated a sense of community around food. Hashtags like #FoodTok and #EasyRecipes bring together millions of users,

fostering creativity and connection. Viewers share their tips, tweaks, and reactions, creating a collaborative culinary space.

- **Focus on Simplicity:** With most videos lasting under a minute, recipes are designed to be quick and straightforward. This focus on simplicity aligns perfectly with today's busy lifestyles, making cooking more manageable without sacrificing flavor.
- **Global Influence:** TikTok has exposed millions to international cuisines and cooking techniques. Dishes from Korea, Italy, Mexico, and beyond have gained popularity, broadening palates and inspiring home cooks to experiment with flavors they might not have encountered otherwise.
- **Fun and Entertainment:** Above all, TikTok has made cooking fun. With quirky edits, catchy soundtracks, and playful commentary, cooking has become less of a chore and more of an experience—one that's meant to be enjoyed and shared.

Tools and Ingredients to Get Started

Before diving into the recipes, let's make sure your kitchen is stocked with the essentials. TikTok recipes often call for simple tools and readily available ingredients, but having a few key items on hand will set you up for success.

Essential Kitchen Tools:

1. **Non-Stick Pan:** A high-quality non-stick pan is a must for many TikTok recipes, from fluffy pancakes to crispy tortilla wraps.
2. **Mixing Bowls:** A set of mixing bowls in various sizes will help you prep ingredients with ease.
3. **Whisk and Spatula:** These tools are essential for mixing batters, scrambling eggs, and flipping foods without breaking them.
4. **Air Fryer:** This trendy gadget has become a TikTok favorite for making everything from crispy chips to healthy desserts.
5. **Blender or Food Processor:** Perfect for making sauces, smoothies, or even viral trends like the Green Goddess Salad.
6. **Baking Tray:** For oven-based recipes like sheet-pan meals or baked snacks.
7. **Sharp Knife and Cutting Board:** Precision and safety are key when chopping, slicing, or dicing.
8. **Measuring Cups and Spoons:** Accuracy is important, especially for baking or replicating viral recipes.

Must-Have Ingredients:

1. **Eggs:** A staple for breakfast trends, quick snacks, and protein-packed meals.
2. **Flour and Baking Essentials:** Perfect for making pancakes, mug cakes, or 3-ingredient baked goods.
3. **Cheese:** From gooey mozzarella to tangy feta, cheese is a star ingredient in many TikTok recipes.
4. **Fresh Herbs and Greens:** Spinach, parsley, coriander, and basil can elevate any dish.
5. **Rice and Pasta:** These pantry staples are the backbone of countless viral recipes, including fried rice and one-pot pasta dishes.
6. **Soy Sauce and Honey:** Common flavor enhancers in both savory and sweet creations.
7. **Avocado:** Perfect for creamy spreads, toppings, and viral breakfast dishes.
8. **Seasonings:** TikTok recipes often rely on simple seasonings like salt, pepper, garlic powder, and chili flakes for bold flavors.

Bonus Items for TikTok Recipes:

- **Tortillas:** Essential for wrap hacks and quesadillas.
- **Nutella or Biscoff Spread:** Ideal for viral desserts and sweet treats.
- **Yoghurt:** A versatile ingredient for breakfasts, desserts, and sauces.
- **Fruit:** Bananas, berries, and apples often take center stage in TikTok's quick and healthy recipes.

With these tools and ingredients in your arsenal, you're ready to jump into the world of TikTok cooking. Remember, the goal isn't perfection—it's about having fun, experimenting, and sharing your creations with others. Let's get started!

BREAKFAST TRENDS

Pancake Cereal Bliss

Prep Time: 10 minutes   **Cook Time:** 15 minutes   **Servings:** 4

Ingredients

- 1 cup (120g) all-purpose flour
- 1 tablespoon granulated sugar
- 1 teaspoon baking powder
- 1/4 teaspoon baking soda
- 1/4 teaspoon salt
- 3/4 cup (180ml) milk
- 1 large egg
- 1 teaspoon vanilla extract
- 1 tablespoon melted butter or neutral oil (plus more for greasing the pan)
- Optional toppings: maple syrup, fresh fruit, whipped cream, chocolate chips

Instructions

1. In a large mixing bowl, whisk together the flour, sugar, baking powder, baking soda, and salt until evenly combined. In a separate bowl, mix the milk, egg, vanilla extract, and melted butter until smooth. Gradually add the wet ingredients to the dry ingredients, stirring until just combined; the batter should be slightly thick and free of large lumps.
2. Heat a non-stick frying pan or griddle over medium heat and lightly grease with butter or oil. Pour the batter into a squeeze bottle or piping bag with a small round tip for easier handling. Pipe small dots of batter onto the pan, about the size of a coin, leaving space between each. Cook for 1–2 minutes until bubbles form on the surface and the edges appear set, then flip with a spatula and cook for another 30 seconds or until golden brown. Repeat until all the batter is used.
3. Serve the pancake cereal in bowls and drizzle with maple syrup. Add your choice of toppings, such as fresh berries, banana slices, or whipped cream, for a personalised touch.

Nutritional Information (Per Serving)

- Calories: 180
- Protein: 5g
- Carbohydrates: 28g
- Fat: 6g
- Saturated Fat: 2g
- Cholesterol: 50mg
- Sodium: 210mg
- Fiber: 1g
- Sugar: 6g

Overnight Weetabix Cheesecake

Prep Time: 15 minutes   **Cook Time:** None (chill overnight)   **Servings:** 2

Ingredients

- **2 Weetabix biscuits**
- **50ml milk (or your preferred milk alternative)**
- **200g low-fat cream cheese**
- **100g Greek yoghurt (plain or vanilla)**
- **2 tablespoons honey or maple syrup**
- **1 teaspoon vanilla extract**
- **4–5 digestive biscuits (crushed)**
- **50g fresh strawberries (or any berry of your choice), chopped**
- **1 tablespoon strawberry jam (optional)**

Instructions

1. Start by crushing the Weetabix biscuits into fine crumbs and mix them with milk until you achieve a slightly moist consistency. Spread this mixture evenly across the bottom of two small jars or ramekins to form the base layer.
2. In a mixing bowl, combine the cream cheese, Greek yoghurt, honey, and vanilla extract. Whisk the mixture until it is smooth and creamy, ensuring no lumps remain. Spoon the cheesecake filling evenly over the Weetabix base, spreading it gently with the back of a spoon to create a flat surface.
3. Sprinkle a layer of crushed digestive biscuits on top of the cheesecake filling for added crunch. Gently press them into place to secure the topping. Cover the jars or ramekins with cling film and refrigerate them overnight to allow the flavors to meld and the cheesecake to set.
4. Before serving, top the cheesecakes with chopped fresh strawberries. If desired, drizzle with a small amount of strawberry jam for added sweetness and a glossy finish. Serve chilled and enjoy this delicious and easy-to-make treat.

Nutritional Information (per serving)

- Calories: 250 kcal
- Protein: 10g
- Carbohydrates: 35g
- Fat: 8g
- Saturated Fat: 4g
- Fiber: 4g
- Sugar: 18g

Cloud Eggs with a Twist

Prep Time: 10 minutes   **Cook Time:** 5 minutes   **Servings:** 2

Ingredients

- **2 large eggs**
- **2 tbsp grated Parmesan cheese**
- **1 tbsp finely chopped fresh chives**
- **1/4 tsp smoked paprika**
- **Salt and pepper, to taste**
- **2 slices of sourdough bread**
- **(optional, for serving)**
- **1 tbsp butter (for toasting bread, optional)**

Instructions

1. Preheat your oven to 220°C (200°C fan) or gas mark 7. Separate the egg whites from the yolks, keeping the yolks intact in individual small bowls. In a clean mixing bowl, whisk the egg whites using an electric mixer or a hand whisk until stiff peaks form.
2. Carefully fold in the grated Parmesan cheese, chopped chives, smoked paprika, and a pinch of salt and pepper without deflating the egg whites. Line a baking tray with parchment paper, then spoon the whipped egg whites into two mounds.
3. Use the back of a spoon to create a small well in the center of each mound. Bake the egg whites in the oven for 3 minutes until slightly firm. Remove from the oven and gently place one yolk into the well of each cloud.
4. Return to the oven and bake for an additional 2 minutes until the yolks are just set. While the eggs are baking, toast the sourdough bread in butter in a hot pan until golden brown. Serve the cloud eggs immediately on their own or on the buttered toast. Garnish with extra chives if desired.

Nutritional Information (Per Serving)

- Calories: 120 (without toast)
- Protein: 8g
- Carbohydrates: 1g
- Fat: 9g
- Fiber: 0g
- Sodium: 150mg

Baked Oats Banana Choc Chip

Prep Time: 10 minutes   **Cook Time:** 25 minutes   **Servings:** 2

Ingredients

- **1 medium ripe banana**
- **80g rolled oats**
- **1 large egg**
- **120ml milk (any type: dairy, almond, or oat)**
- **1 tsp baking powder**
- **1 tsp vanilla extract**
- **1 tbsp maple syrup or honey (optional)**
- **30g dark chocolate chips**
- **A pinch of salt**
- **Cooking spray or butter for greasing**

Instructions

1. Mash the ripe banana in a mixing bowl until smooth. Add the rolled oats, egg, milk, baking powder, vanilla extract, and a pinch of salt to the bowl. Stir well until the mixture is fully combined and smooth. For additional sweetness, you can add maple syrup or honey at this stage.
2. Preheat your oven to 180°C (fan) or 200°C (conventional). Grease a small baking dish or two ramekins with cooking spray or a thin layer of butter to prevent sticking. Pour the mixture into the prepared dish(es) and spread evenly. Sprinkle the dark chocolate chips on top or fold them into the batter for a melty surprise inside.
3. Place the dish in the preheated oven and bake for 20–25 minutes, or until the top is golden brown and the oats are set. Remove from the oven and let it cool for a few minutes before serving.
4. Serve warm with a drizzle of honey, fresh banana slices, or a dollop of yoghurt if desired.

Nutritional Information (Per Serving)

- Calories: 275 kcal
- Protein: 9g
- Carbohydrates: 40g
- Sugar: 12g
- Fiber: 5g
- Fat: 8g
- Saturated Fat: 3g
- Salt: 0.2g

Croissant Cereal Delight

Prep Time: 10 minutes   **Cook Time:** 10 minutes   **Servings:** 4

Ingredients

- **4 mini croissants**
- **2 tbsp unsalted butter, melted**
- **2 tbsp granulated sugar**
- **1 tsp ground cinnamon**
- **250ml whole milk (or your preferred milk)**
- **Optional toppings: fresh berries, honey, or chocolate chips**

Instructions

1. Preheat your oven to 180°C (fan) or 200°C (conventional). Slice each mini croissant into small bite-sized pieces, roughly the size of cereal. Place the croissant pieces on a baking tray lined with parchment paper. Drizzle the melted butter over the croissant pieces, ensuring each piece is lightly coated. In a small bowl, mix the sugar and cinnamon together, then sprinkle the mixture evenly over the buttered croissant pieces. Toss gently to coat.
2. Bake the croissant pieces in the preheated oven for 8-10 minutes, or until they are golden and crisp. Keep a close eye on them to prevent burning. Remove the tray from the oven and let the croissant cereal cool slightly. Once cooled, transfer to bowls and

pour milk over the croissant cereal. Add optional toppings like fresh berries, honey, or chocolate chips for extra flavour. Serve immediately and enjoy the delightful crunch of your homemade croissant cereal.

Nutritional Information (Per Serving)

- Calories: 225 kcal
- Fat: 12g
- Saturated Fat: 7g
- Carbohydrates: 24g
- Sugars: 8g
- Protein: 4g
- Fiber: 1g
- Salt: 0.2g

Savoury Breakfast Mug Cake

Prep Time: 5 minutes   **Cook Time:** 2 minutes   **Servings:** 1

Ingredients:

- **2 large eggs**
- **2 tbsp milk (whole or semi-skimmed)**
- **2 tbsp grated cheese (cheddar or your choice)**
- **2 tbsp whole wheat flour**
- **1/4 tsp baking powder**
- **1/4 tsp garlic powder**
- **1/4 tsp dried mixed herbs (such as oregano and thyme)**
- **Salt and pepper to taste**
- **1 tbsp cooked spinach (optional, for extra greens)**
- **1 tbsp cooked ham or bacon bits (optional)**

Instructions:

1. In a microwave-safe mug, whisk the eggs and milk together until fully combined. Add the flour, baking powder, garlic powder, dried herbs, salt, and pepper, then mix until smooth. Stir in the grated cheese, spinach, and ham or bacon bits if using. Microwave the mixture on high for 1-2 minutes, checking at the 1-minute mark to see if it has risen and cooked through. If necessary, microwave in 15-second intervals until fully cooked. Once done, let it cool slightly before enjoying.

Nutritional Info (Per Serving):

- Calories: 300 kcal
- Protein: 20g
- Carbohydrates: 10g
- Fat: 20g
- Fiber: 2g
- Sugar: 2g
- Sodium: 400mg

Maple Syrup Stuffed French Toast

Prep Time: 10 minutes   **Cook Time:** 15 minutes   **Servings:** 4

Ingredients:

- 8 slices of thick-cut white or wholemeal bread
- 4 large eggs
- 200ml whole milk
- 2 tbsp vanilla extract
- 1 tsp ground cinnamon
- 2 tbsp butter (for frying)
- 4 tbsp maple syrup (for stuffing)
- 2 tbsp icing sugar (for dusting)
- Fresh berries or whipped cream (optional, for serving)

Instructions:

1. Start by whisking the eggs, milk, vanilla extract, and ground cinnamon together in a large mixing bowl until smooth.
2. Next, spread maple syrup onto 4 slices of bread and top each with another slice of bread to form sandwiches.
3. Heat a frying pan or griddle over medium heat and melt the butter.
4. Dip each sandwich into the egg mixture, ensuring both sides are coated, and place it into the hot pan. Cook for about 3-4 minutes on each side, or until golden brown and crispy.
5. Once all French toast sandwiches are cooked, dust them with icing sugar and serve with fresh berries or whipped cream, if desired.

Nutritional Info (per serving):

- Calories: 350 kcal
- Protein: 8g
- Carbohydrates: 48g
- Sugars: 24g
- Fat: 14g
- Saturated Fat: 7g
- Fiber: 2g
- Salt: 0.5g

Breakfast Bagel Sliders

Prep Time: 10 minutes   **Cook Time:** 15 minutes   **Servings:** 4 sliders

Ingredients

- 4 mini bagels (whole wheat or plain)
- 4 large eggs
- 4 slices of cooked bacon
- 2 slices of cheddar cheese
- 1 tablespoon butter
- 1 tablespoon mayonnaise
- 1 teaspoon Dijon mustard
- 1 teaspoon fresh chives, chopped
- Salt and pepper, to taste
- Optional: Spinach or arugula for added greens

Instructions

1. Start by splitting the mini bagels in half and toasting them lightly in a toaster or on a dry skillet for about 1-2 minutes until golden and crisp.

2. In a small bowl, mix together the mayonnaise, Dijon mustard, and chopped chives to create a spread for the bagels. Season with salt and pepper to taste.
3. In a skillet, heat the butter over medium heat. Crack the eggs into the pan and cook to your preference (fried sunny side up or scrambled). Season with salt and pepper as needed.
4. While the eggs cook, heat the bacon slices in a separate pan or in the microwave until crispy.
5. Once the eggs are done, place a slice of cheddar cheese on top of each egg and let it melt for about 1 minute.
6. To assemble the sliders, spread the chive mayo on the bottom half of each toasted mini bagel. Layer with a slice of bacon, followed by the cheesy egg, and top with the other bagel half.
7. Serve warm with optional greens like spinach or arugula for added freshness.

Nutritional Information (Per Slider)

- Calories: 350 kcal
- Protein: 18g
- Carbohydrates: 27g
- Fat: 21g
- Saturated Fat: 9g
- Fiber: 3g
- Sugar: 3g
- Sodium: 580mg

Rolled Egg Sandwich

Prep Time: 10 minutes   **Cook Time:** 5 minutes   **Servings:** 2

Ingredients:
- **4 large eggs**
- **2 slices of whole wheat or white bread**
- **1 tablespoon mayonnaise**
- **1 teaspoon Dijon mustard**
- **Salt and pepper, to taste**
- **Fresh parsley (optional, for garnish)**
- **1 tablespoon butter**
- **A pinch of paprika (optional)**

Instructions:
1. Start by boiling the eggs. In a saucepan, bring water to a boil and gently lower the eggs in. Boil them for 8 minutes for hard-boiled eggs. Once done, remove the eggs and let them cool under cold running water before peeling.
2. Next, place the eggs in a bowl and mash them with a fork until they are crumbled into small pieces. Add mayonnaise, Dijon mustard, salt, and pepper to the eggs and mix well.
3. In the meantime, toast the slices of bread until golden and crispy.
4. Spread a thin layer of butter on one side of each slice of bread.

5. Once the bread is toasted, evenly distribute the egg mixture onto one slice of bread. Roll the slice of bread tightly, creating a sandwich roll.
6. Cut the rolled sandwich into halves or smaller pieces, depending on your preference. Garnish with fresh parsley and a sprinkle of paprika for extra flavor and color.

Nutritional Information (per serving):

- Calories: 310 kcal
- Protein: 14g
- Carbohydrates: 28g
- Sugars: 4g
- Fat: 18g
- Saturated Fat: 6g
- Fiber: 3g
- Salt: 1g

Air Fryer Hash Brown Tacos

Prep Time: 10 minutes   **Cook Time:** 15 minutes   **Servings:** 4

Ingredients:

- **4 hash brown patties (frozen or homemade)**
- **1 tbsp olive oil (or cooking spray)**
- **1 cup cooked chicken breast, shredded (optional)**
- **½ cup cheddar cheese, shredded**
- **¼ cup sour cream or Greek yogurt**
- **1 ripe avocado, sliced**
- **½ cup lettuce, shredded**
- **2 tbsp salsa or pico de gallo**
- **1 tbsp chopped fresh coriander (optional)**
- **Salt and pepper, to taste**

Instructions:

1. Preheat the air fryer to 180°C (350°F).
2. Lightly spray the hash brown patties with olive oil or cooking spray.
3. Place the hash brown patties in the air fryer basket in a single layer. Cook for 10-12 minutes, flipping halfway through, until golden and crispy.
4. While the hash browns are cooking, prepare the taco toppings: shred the lettuce, slice the avocado, and prepare the salsa or pico de gallo.
5. Once the hash browns are cooked, remove them from the air fryer and allow them to cool slightly.
6. Carefully cut each hash brown in half, creating a taco shell shape.
7. Place the hash brown taco shells on a serving plate. Start with a layer of shredded chicken (if using), followed by cheese, lettuce, avocado slices, and a dollop of sour cream or Greek yogurt.
8. Top with salsa or pico de gallo and a sprinkle of fresh coriander.
9. Season with salt and pepper to taste.
10. Serve immediately and enjoy!

TikTok Folded Egg Wrap

Prep Time: 5 minutes   **Cook Time:** 5 minutes   **Servings:** 1

Ingredients

- **2 large eggs**
- **1 tbsp butter or olive oil**
- **1 large flour tortilla**
- **Salt and pepper, to taste**
- **2 tbsp grated cheese (cheddar, mozzarella, or your choice)**
- **1/4 avocado, sliced (optional)**
- **Fresh herbs (e.g., chives or parsley), chopped (optional)**

Instructions

1. In a bowl, crack the eggs and whisk them together with a pinch of salt and pepper.
2. Heat the butter or olive oil in a non-stick frying pan over medium heat.
3. Pour the beaten eggs into the pan and let them cook without stirring. As the eggs begin to set, use a spatula to gently push the edges toward the centre, allowing the uncooked egg to flow to the sides.
4. Once the eggs are mostly set but still slightly runny, carefully flip them over. Cook for another 30 seconds until fully set. Remove from the heat.
5. While the eggs are cooking, warm the tortilla in a separate pan or microwave for 10-20 seconds to make it more pliable.
6. Place the tortilla on a flat surface, and then add the cooked folded eggs on one side.
7. Sprinkle the grated cheese on top of the eggs, followed by the avocado slices and herbs (if using).
8. Fold the tortilla over the egg mixture, creating a neat wrap. You can fold in the sides slightly to secure the contents.
9. Optionally, place the wrap back in the pan for 1-2 minutes to crisp up and melt the cheese.
10. Slice the wrap in half and serve immediately.

Nutritional Info (per serving)

- Calories: 345 kcal
- Protein: 16g
- Fat: 23g
- Saturated fat: 9g
- Carbohydrates: 22g
- Sugars: 2g
- Fibre: 4g
- Sodium: 400mg

Avocado & Egg Pancakes

Prep Time: 10 minutes   **Cook Time:** 10 minutes   **Servings:** 2

Ingredients:

- **1 ripe avocado**
- **2 large eggs**
- **2 tablespoons wholemeal flour**
- **1/4 teaspoon baking powder**
- **Salt and pepper to taste**
- **1 tablespoon olive oil (for cooking)**
- **Fresh herbs (optional, for garnish)**
- **A dollop of Greek yoghurt (optional, for serving)**

Instructions:

1. Start by mashing the ripe avocado in a bowl until smooth. Add the eggs to the mashed avocado and whisk until well combined. Stir in the wholemeal flour and baking powder, mixing until the batter comes together. Season with a pinch of salt and pepper to taste.

2. Heat the olive oil in a non-stick frying pan over medium heat. Once the pan is hot, pour small amounts of the batter into the pan to form pancakes, using the back of a spoon to spread them out evenly. Cook each pancake for about 2–3 minutes on one side, or until bubbles form on top and the edges start to look set. Flip the pancake and cook for another 1–2 minutes until golden and cooked through.

3. Serve the pancakes hot, garnished with fresh herbs if desired. Add a dollop of Greek yoghurt on top for extra creaminess. Enjoy!

Nutritional Info (per serving):

- Calories: 350 kcal
- Protein: 13g
- Carbohydrates: 23g
- Fats: 22g
- Fiber: 8g
- Sugar: 2g
- Sodium: 250mg

Cinnamon Roll Pancakes

Prep Time: 15 minutes   **Cook Time:** 10 minutes   **Servings:** 4

Ingredients

For the Pancakes

- 200g self-raising flour
- 1 tablespoon baking powder
- 1/2 teaspoon salt
- 2 tablespoons sugar
- 2 large eggs
- 240ml whole milk
- 1 teaspoon vanilla extract
- 1 tablespoon unsalted butter, melted

For the Cinnamon Swirl

- 60g unsalted butter, melted
- 100g soft brown sugar
- 2 teaspoons ground cinnamon

For the Glaze

- 100g icing sugar
- 2 tablespoons milk
- 1/2 teaspoon vanilla extract

Instructions

1. For the pancakes, whisk together the flour, baking powder, salt, and sugar in a large bowl. In another bowl, whisk the eggs, milk, vanilla extract, and melted butter. Pour the wet ingredients into the dry ingredients and stir until just combined. The batter should be thick but pourable. If it's too thick, add a bit more milk to achieve the desired consistency.
2. In a small bowl, combine the melted butter, brown sugar, and cinnamon to create the cinnamon swirl mixture.
3. Preheat a non-stick frying pan or griddle over medium heat and lightly grease it with butter or oil. Pour a small ladle of pancake batter onto the pan, spreading it out into a round shape. Using a spoon or piping bag, drizzle the cinnamon swirl mixture over the pancake in a swirl pattern. Allow it to cook for 2-3 minutes, then flip it over and cook for another 2-3 minutes on the other side, until golden and cooked through.
4. Repeat the process with the remaining batter, making sure to grease the pan between each batch.
5. For the glaze, whisk together the icing sugar, milk, and vanilla extract until smooth. Drizzle over the warm pancakes before serving.

Nutritional Information (per serving)

- Calories: 410 kcal
- Fat: 20g
- Saturated Fat: 12g
- Carbohydrates: 55g
- Sugars: 30g
- Protein: 5g
- Fibre: 1g
- Salt: 0.6g

Mini Full English Bites

Prep Time: 15 minutes   **Cook Time:** 25 minutes   **Servings:** 4

Ingredients:

- **8 small sausages (preferably pork or chicken)**
- **8 small rashers of back bacon**
- **4 eggs**
- **8 cherry tomatoes, halved**
- **8 button mushrooms, sliced**
- **8 mini hash browns**
- **4 slices of black pudding (optional)**
- **2 tbsp olive oil**
- **Salt and pepper to taste**
- **1 tbsp fresh parsley, chopped (for garnish)**

Instructions:

1. Preheat the oven to 200°C (180°C fan)/400°F.
2. In a large baking tray, place the sausages, bacon, cherry tomatoes (cut side up), mushrooms, and black pudding (if using). Drizzle with olive oil and season with salt and pepper.

3. Roast in the oven for 15-20 minutes or until the sausages are cooked through and the bacon is crispy.
4. While the ingredients are roasting, heat a non-stick frying pan over medium heat. Cook the hash browns according to the package instructions, then set aside.
5. In the same pan, fry the eggs to your desired doneness (sunny side up, scrambled, or fried).
6. Once everything is cooked, arrange the sausages, bacon, mushrooms, tomatoes, black pudding, hash browns, and eggs onto serving plates.
7. Garnish with fresh parsley and serve immediately.

Nutritional Info (per serving):
- Calories: 450 kcal
- Carbs: 15g
- Protein: 28g
- Fat: 32g
- Saturated Fat: 10g
- Fibre: 3g
- Sugar: 4g
- Salt: 1.2g

Peanut Butter Banana Chia Pudding

Prep Time: 5 minutes **Cook Time:** 0 minutes **Servings:** 2

Ingredients:
- 2 ripe bananas, mashed
- 2 tbsp peanut butter (smooth or crunchy)
- 1 cup unsweetened almond milk (or milk of choice)
- 3 tbsp chia seeds
- 1 tsp vanilla extract
- 1 tbsp honey or maple syrup (optional for sweetness)
- Pinch of salt
- Sliced bananas, chopped peanuts, and a drizzle of peanut butter (for topping)

Instructions:
1. In a medium-sized bowl, mash the bananas until smooth.
   Stir in the peanut butter, almond milk, and vanilla extract. Mix well until the peanut butter is fully combined with the milk.
2. Add the chia seeds, honey (if using), and a pinch of salt, and stir everything together.
3. Cover the bowl with a lid or plastic wrap and place it in the fridge for at least 2 hours or overnight to allow the chia seeds to absorb the liquid and thicken the mixture.
4. Once ready to serve, give the pudding a good stir. Divide it into two bowls or glasses.
5. Top with sliced bananas, chopped peanuts, and a drizzle of peanut butter for extra flavour and texture.
6. Enjoy!

Nutritional Info (per serving):

- Calories: 290 kcal
- Protein: 7g
- Carbohydrates: 35g
- Sugars: 15g
- Fibre: 7g
- Fat: 14g
- Saturated fat: 2g
- Sodium: 120mg
- Calcium: 250mg
- Iron: 1.5mg

Spinach and Feta Breakfast Wrap

Prep Time: 10 minutes   **Cook Time:** 5 minutes   **Servings:** 2

Ingredients

- **4 large eggs**
- **1 cup of fresh spinach, roughly chopped**
- **100g feta cheese, crumbled**
- **2 large flour tortillas**
- **Salt and pepper, to taste**
- **Butter or oil for cooking**

Instructions

1. Start by heating a small amount of butter or oil in a frying pan over medium heat. Add the chopped spinach and sauté for 2-3 minutes, until the spinach is wilted.
2. Remove it from the pan and set it aside. In the same pan, crack the eggs into a bowl and season with salt and pepper. Whisk them together and pour them into the pan, scrambling gently as they cook for 3-4 minutes until fully cooked. Once the eggs are done, remove them from the pan.
3. Next, lay a tortilla flat on a surface and evenly spread half of the scrambled eggs across one half of the tortilla. Top with half of the cooked spinach and crumbled feta cheese.
4. Fold the tortilla in half to cover the filling. Return the pan to the heat, and cook the wrap for about 2-3 minutes on each side until the tortilla becomes golden brown and crispy. Repeat with the second tortilla.
5. Finally, slice each wrap in half and serve immediately.

Nutritional Information (per serving)

- Calories: 350 kcal
- Total Fat: 18g
- Saturated Fat: 8g
- Carbohydrates: 27g
- Protein: 15g
- Fiber: 3g
- Sugar: 3g
- Salt: 500mg

Rainbow Smoothie Parfait

Prep Time: 10 minutes   **Cook Time:** 0 minutes   **Servings:** 2

Ingredients

- 1 cup frozen mixed berries (blueberries, strawberries, raspberries)
- 1 cup frozen mango chunks
- 1 cup frozen pineapple chunks
- 1 cup Greek yogurt
- 1 tbsp honey (optional)
- 1/2 cup coconut water or almond milk
- 1 tbsp chia seeds
- Fresh fruit for topping (e.g. kiwi, banana slices, berries)

Instructions

1. Start by making each layer of the smoothie. For the first layer, blend the frozen mixed berries with 1/2 cup of coconut water or almond milk and a tablespoon of honey (if using) until smooth.
2. Set aside in a bowl. For the second layer, blend the frozen mango chunks with another 1/2 cup of coconut water or almond milk until smooth and set aside. For the third layer, blend the frozen pineapple chunks with the remaining coconut water or almond milk until smooth.
3. Next, prepare your parfait glasses. Layer the smoothie mixture, starting with the berry layer at the bottom, followed by the mango layer, and then the pineapple layer. Add a dollop of Greek yogurt on top of the layers.
4. Top the parfait with chia seeds and fresh fruit for decoration. You can use slices of kiwi, banana, or more berries for a vibrant touch. Serve immediately and enjoy the colourful, nutritious treat.

Nutritional Information (per serving)

- Calories: 210 kcal
- Total Fat: 4g
- Saturated Fat: 1g
- Carbohydrates: 38g
- Protein: 8g
- Fiber: 5g
- Sugar: 23g
- Salt: 35mg

Whipped Ricotta Toast

Prep Time: 5 minutes   **Cook Time:** 3 minutes   **Servings:** 2

Ingredients

- 200g ricotta cheese
- 2 tablespoons honey or maple syrup
- 1 teaspoon vanilla extract
- 2 slices of sourdough or your preferred bread
- 1 tablespoon olive oil
- Fresh fruit (such as berries, figs, or peaches) for topping
- A sprinkle of sea salt
- Fresh mint leaves for garnish (optional)

Instructions

1. To prepare the whipped ricotta, add the ricotta cheese, honey or maple syrup, and vanilla extract into a food processor or blender. Blend until smooth and fluffy, about 1-2 minutes.

2. While the ricotta is being whipped, heat a griddle or non-stick frying pan over medium heat and drizzle the olive oil. Toast the slices of bread on each side for 2-3 minutes, or until golden and crispy.

3. Once the bread is toasted, spread a generous amount of whipped ricotta on top of each slice. Top with fresh fruit of your choice, a light sprinkle of sea salt, and garnish with fresh mint if desired. Serve immediately.

Nutritional Information (per serving)

- Calories: 300 kcal
- Total Fat: 16g
- Saturated Fat: 5g
- Carbohydrates: 27g
- Protein: 12g
- Fiber: 3g
- Sugar: 10g
- Salt: 300mg

Caramelised Banana Toast

Prep Time: 5 minutes   **Cook Time:** 5 minutes   **Servings:** 2

Ingredients

- **2 slices of wholegrain or white bread**
- **1 ripe banana, sliced**
- **1 tablespoon butter**
- **1 tablespoon brown sugar**
- **1 teaspoon cinnamon**
- **1 teaspoon honey (optional)**
- **Pinch of salt**
- **A handful of chopped nuts (e.g., walnuts or pecans) for garnish (optional)**

Instructions

1. Start by toasting the bread until golden and crispy. While the bread is toasting, heat the butter in a frying pan over medium heat until melted. Add the banana slices to the pan and sprinkle over the brown sugar and cinnamon. Cook for 2-3 minutes, gently turning the banana slices to ensure both sides caramelise evenly.

2. Once the banana slices are golden and caramelised, remove the pan from the heat. Drizzle honey (if using) over the bananas for extra sweetness and a shiny finish. Spread the caramelised bananas over the toasted bread slices. Sprinkle a pinch of salt over the top to enhance the sweetness. For added crunch, garnish with chopped nuts if desired.

3. Serve the caramelised banana toast immediately, either as a quick breakfast or a sweet snack.

Nutritional Information (per serving)

- Calories: 250 kcal
- Total Fat: 9g
- Saturated Fat: 5g

- Carbohydrates: 40g
- Protein: 3g
- Fiber: 4g
- Sugar: 20g
- Salt: 220mg

Fluffy Japanese Soufflé Pancakes

Prep Time: 15 minutes **Cook Time:** 15 minutes **Servings:** 2

Ingredients

- **2 large eggs, separated**
- **50g all-purpose flour**
- **2 tablespoons caster sugar**
- **1/2 teaspoon vanilla extract**
- **1/2 teaspoon baking powder**
- **60ml milk**
- **1 tablespoon vegetable oil (for greasing)**
- **Powdered sugar, for dusting**
- **Maple syrup, for serving (optional)**
- **Fresh fruit, for garnish (optional)**

Instructions

1. Begin by whisking the egg whites in a clean bowl until stiff peaks form. In a separate bowl, whisk together the egg yolks, milk, and vanilla extract. Sift in the flour, baking powder, and caster sugar, then mix until smooth.
2. Next, gently fold the egg whites into the yolk mixture in stages, being careful not to deflate the egg whites. The mixture should be fluffy and light.
3. Heat a non-stick frying pan over low heat and lightly grease it with vegetable oil. Spoon the pancake batter onto the pan in 2 to 3 large rounds, using about 2-3 tablespoons of batter per pancake. Cover the pan with a lid and cook for 4-5 minutes, then flip the pancakes carefully and cook for another 3-4 minutes. The pancakes should be puffed and golden brown on both sides.
4. Once cooked, carefully remove the pancakes from the pan and stack them on a plate. Dust with powdered sugar, drizzle with maple syrup, and garnish with fresh fruit if desired. Serve immediately while hot.

Nutritional Information (per serving)

- Calories: 300 kcal
- Total Fat: 14g
- Saturated Fat: 2g
- Carbohydrates: 35g
- Protein: 8g
- Fiber: 1g
- Sugar: 16g
- Salt: 100mg

Jam and Cream Doughnut Toasties

Prep Time: 10 minutes **Cook Time:** 5 minutes **Servings:** 2

Ingredients

- 4 slices of white or wholemeal bread
- 2 tbsp butter, softened
- 4 tbsp jam (strawberry or raspberry works well)
- 4 tbsp clotted cream or thick double cream
- 2 tbsp icing sugar (for dusting)
- 1 tsp vanilla extract (optional)

Instructions

1. Butter each slice of bread on one side. Spread jam on the unbuttered side of two slices and top with clotted cream or double cream. Place the remaining slices of bread on top, buttered side up, to make two sandwiches.
2. Heat a non-stick frying pan over medium heat. Place the sandwiches in the pan and cook for about 2-3 minutes on each side, pressing down gently with a spatula until golden brown and crispy. Once the sandwiches are cooked, remove them from the pan and let them cool for a minute.
3. Once slightly cooled, dust with icing sugar and serve immediately. For an extra touch, you can drizzle a little vanilla extract over the cream before serving.

Nutritional Information (per serving)

- Calories: 400 kcal
- Total Fat: 22g
- Saturated Fat: 12g
- Carbohydrates: 43g
- Sugar: 22g
- Protein: 6g
- Fiber: 2g
- Salt: 0.5g

Apple Pie Breakfast Bowl

Prep Time: 10 minutes   **Cook Time:** 5 minutes   **Servings:** 2

Ingredients

- 2 medium apples, peeled, cored, and chopped
- 1 tbsp butter
- 1 tsp ground cinnamon
- 1/4 tsp ground nutmeg
- 1 tbsp maple syrup (or honey)
- 1/2 cup rolled oats
- 1 cup milk (or dairy-free alternative)
- 1 tbsp chia seeds (optional)
- 2 tbsp chopped walnuts or pecans (optional)
- Greek yogurt or dairy-free yogurt for topping (optional)

Instructions

1. In a medium saucepan, melt butter over medium heat. Add the chopped apples and cook for about 3-4 minutes, stirring occasionally, until they begin to soften. Sprinkle in

the cinnamon and nutmeg, then drizzle in the maple syrup, stirring to coat the apples evenly. Cook for another 1-2 minutes, until the apples are tender and caramelised, then remove from the heat.

2. In a separate saucepan, combine the rolled oats, milk, and chia seeds (if using). Bring to a simmer over medium heat, stirring occasionally, until the oats are cooked and the mixture has thickened, about 3-4 minutes.

3. Once the oats are ready, divide them into two bowls. Top each bowl with the spiced apples, then sprinkle with chopped walnuts or pecans for added crunch, if desired. Add a dollop of Greek yogurt on top for creaminess, and drizzle with a little extra maple syrup if preferred.

4. Serve immediately and enjoy a warm, comforting breakfast.

Nutritional Information (per serving)

- Calories: 350 kcal
- Total Fat: 18g
- Saturated Fat: 5g
- Carbohydrates: 45g
- Protein: 6g
- Fiber: 6g
- Sugar: 20g
- Salt: 40mg

Veggie Packed Savoury Muffins

Prep Time: 15 minutes   **Cook Time:** 20 minutes   **Servings:** 12 muffins

Ingredients

- **200g plain flour**
- **1 tsp baking powder**
- **1/2 tsp baking soda**
- **1/2 tsp salt**
- **1/4 tsp black pepper**
- **1 tsp dried mixed herbs (optional)**
- **2 large eggs**
- **150ml milk (or dairy-free alternative)**
- **50ml olive oil**
- **100g grated carrot**
- **100g courgette, grated**
- **50g sweetcorn (fresh or frozen)**
- **50g red pepper, finely chopped**
- **50g spinach, chopped**
- **50g grated cheddar cheese (optional)**

Instructions

1. In a large bowl, mix the flour, baking powder, baking soda, salt, pepper, and dried herbs (if using). In another bowl, whisk the eggs, milk, and olive oil together until well combined.

2. Add the grated carrot, courgette, sweetcorn, red pepper, and spinach to the wet ingredients, stirring gently to combine. Gradually fold the wet ingredients into the dry ingredients, mixing until just combined.

3. Be careful not to overmix the batter. Spoon the mixture into a lined or greased muffin tin, filling each cup about 2/3 full.

4. Sprinkle the grated cheese on top of each muffin (if using). Bake at 180°C (160°C fan) or 350°F for 20 minutes, or until a toothpick inserted into the centre comes out clean. Let the muffins cool for a few minutes before serving.

Nutritional Information (per muffin)

- Calories: 170 kcal
- Total Fat: 9g
- Saturated Fat: 1.5g
- Carbohydrates: 19g
- Protein: 4g
- Fiber: 2g
- Sugar: 4g
- Salt: 200mg

TikTok Cheddar Waffle Sandwich

Prep Time: 5 minutes   **Cook Time:** 5 minutes   **Servings:** 2

Ingredients

- **4 slices of bread (preferably thick-cut white or wholemeal)**
- **100g cheddar cheese, grated**
- **2 tbsp unsalted butter, softened**
- **2 tsp Dijon mustard (optional)**
- **Salt and pepper, to taste**

Instructions

1. Butter one side of each slice of bread. Spread a thin layer of Dijon mustard (if using) on the unbuttered side of two slices. Place the grated cheddar cheese evenly over the mustard side of the bread.
2. Top with the remaining slices of bread, buttered side out, to form two sandwiches.
3. Heat a waffle maker according to the manufacturer's instructions. Once hot, place the sandwiches in the waffle maker, close the lid, and cook for about 3-5 minutes, or until the bread is golden brown and the cheese is melted. Remove the sandwiches from the waffle maker and slice in half.
4. Serve immediately while the cheese is still gooey and the bread is crispy.

Nutritional Information (per serving)

- Calories: 400 kcal
- Total Fat: 25g
- Saturated Fat: 12g
- Carbohydrates: 32g
- Protein: 16g
- Fiber: 2g
- Sugar: 3g
- Salt: 650mg

Porridge Bars with Berries

Prep Time: 10 minutes   **Cook Time:** 20 minutes   **Servings:** 12 bars

Ingredients

- **200g rolled oats**
- **200ml milk (dairy or plant-based)**
- **2 tablespoons honey or maple syrup**
- **1 teaspoon vanilla extract**

- 1/2 teaspoon ground cinnamon
- 1/4 teaspoon salt
- 100g mixed berries (fresh or frozen)
- 50g almonds or walnuts, chopped (optional)
- 1 tablespoon chia seeds (optional)
- 2 tablespoons coconut oil or butter, melted

Instructions

1. Preheat the oven to 180°C (160°C fan) or 350°F. Line a square baking tin (around 8-inch/20cm) with parchment paper. In a mixing bowl, combine the rolled oats, ground cinnamon, and salt.

2. In a separate bowl, whisk together the milk, honey (or maple syrup), vanilla extract, and melted coconut oil or butter. Pour the wet ingredients into the dry ingredients and stir until everything is well combined.

3. Gently fold in the mixed berries, chopped nuts, and chia seeds if using. Pour the mixture into the prepared baking tin, spreading it out evenly. Bake in the preheated oven for 18-20 minutes, or until the edges are golden and the centre is set. Allow the bars to cool in the tin for 10 minutes before transferring them to a wire rack to cool completely. Once cool, slice into 12 bars and store in an airtight container for up to 5 days.

Nutritional Information (per bar)

- Calories: 180 kcal
- Total Fat: 8g
- Saturated Fat: 3g
- Carbohydrates: 25g
- Protein: 4g
- Fiber: 3g
- Sugar: 8g
- Salt: 0.1g

Snack & Appetizer Hacks

Feta Pasta Chips

Prep Time: 10 minutes   **Cook Time:** 20 minutes   **Servings:** 4

Ingredients

- 250g penne pasta
- 200g feta cheese
- 2 tablespoons olive oil
- 1 teaspoon garlic powder
- 1 teaspoon dried oregano
- 1/2 teaspoon paprika
- Salt and pepper, to taste
- Fresh parsley (optional, for garnish)

Instructions

1. Preheat the oven to 200°C (180°C fan) or 400°F. Cook the penne pasta according to the package instructions, until al dente. Drain and set aside.
2. On a baking tray, place the block of feta cheese in the centre and surround it with the cooked pasta. Drizzle olive oil over the pasta and feta, then sprinkle with garlic powder, oregano, paprika, salt, and pepper.
3. Toss the pasta gently to coat. Bake in the preheated oven for 15-20 minutes, or until the feta is golden and the pasta is crispy. Once baked, remove from the oven and carefully stir the pasta and feta together to combine. Serve immediately, garnished with fresh parsley if desired.

Nutritional Information (per serving)

- Calories: 350 kcal
- Total Fat: 18g
- Saturated Fat: 6g
- Carbohydrates: 38g
- Protein: 12g
- Fiber: 2g
- Sugar: 2g
- Salt: 800mg

Rice Paper Bacon Rolls

Prep Time: 10 minutes   **Cook Time:** 15 minutes   **Servings:** 4

Ingredients

- 8 slices of bacon
- 8 rice paper sheets
- 1 tablespoon olive oil
- 1 teaspoon smoked paprika (optional)
- 1 tablespoon maple syrup (optional)

- Fresh herbs (such as parsley or thyme) for garnish

Instructions

1. Start by heating a frying pan over medium heat. Add the bacon slices and cook them until crispy, about 5-7 minutes. Once done, remove the bacon and set it on paper towels to drain any excess fat.
2. Allow it to cool slightly. While the bacon is cooling, prepare a shallow bowl of warm water to soak the rice paper sheets. Submerge one rice paper sheet at a time into the water for about 10-15 seconds, or until it becomes soft and pliable.
3. Lay the softened rice paper on a clean, flat surface. Place one slice of cooked bacon in the centre of the rice paper. Optionally, drizzle a small amount of maple syrup and sprinkle smoked paprika over the bacon for extra flavour.
4. Carefully fold the sides of the rice paper over the bacon and then roll it up tightly, ensuring the bacon is fully encased. Repeat this process for the remaining bacon slices.
5. Once all rolls are prepared, heat the olive oil in a frying pan over medium heat. Place the rice paper rolls in the pan and cook them for 2-3 minutes on each side, or until golden and crispy.
6. Once done, remove the rolls from the pan and place them on a plate lined with paper towels to remove any excess oil. Garnish with fresh herbs and serve immediately.

Nutritional Information (per serving)

- Calories: 250 kcal
- Total Fat: 18g
- Saturated Fat: 6g
- Carbohydrates: 10g
- Protein: 12g
- Fiber: 1g
- Sugar: 2g
- Salt: 600mg

Tortilla Pinwheel Wraps

Prep Time: 15 minutes   **Cook Time:** 0 minutes   **Servings:** 4

Ingredients

- 4 large flour tortillas
- 100g cream cheese, softened
- 2 tbsp mayonnaise
- 1 tsp Dijon mustard
- 1 tbsp fresh chives, chopped
- 1 tbsp fresh parsley, chopped
- 150g cooked chicken breast, shredded
- 75g sliced ham
- 50g cheddar cheese, grated
- 1 small cucumber, thinly sliced
- 1 small red bell pepper, thinly sliced
- Salt and pepper, to taste

Instructions

1. Spread the cream cheese evenly over each tortilla. In a bowl, mix the mayonnaise, Dijon mustard, chopped chives, parsley, salt, and pepper.
2. Spread this mixture on top of the cream cheese. Layer the shredded chicken, sliced ham, grated cheddar cheese, cucumber, and red bell pepper evenly on the tortillas.
3. Tightly roll up each tortilla, ensuring the filling stays in place. Slice the rolled tortillas into 1-inch wide pinwheels. Arrange the pinwheels on a serving platter and serve immediately or refrigerate until ready to serve.

Nutritional Information (per serving)

- Calories: 310 kcal
- Total Fat: 18g
- Saturated Fat: 7g
- Carbohydrates: 21g
- Protein: 15g
- Fiber: 3g
- Sugar: 4g
- Salt: 650mg

Crispy Cheesy Potato Sticks

Prep Time: 15 minutes   **Cook Time:** 25 minutes   **Servings:** 4

Ingredients

- **4 medium potatoes, peeled and cut into thin sticks**
- **100g cheddar cheese, grated**
- **2 tablespoons all-purpose flour**
- **1 large egg, beaten**
- **2 tablespoons breadcrumbs**
- **1 teaspoon garlic powder**
- **1 teaspoon paprika**
- **Salt and pepper, to taste**
- **Olive oil spray for cooking**

Instructions

1. Preheat your oven to 200°C (180°C fan) or 400°F. Line a baking tray with parchment paper.
2. In a large bowl, toss the potato sticks with a small drizzle of olive oil, salt, and pepper. Spread them out evenly on the prepared baking tray and bake for 15-20 minutes, flipping halfway through, until the potatoes are soft and golden but not fully crispy.
3. While the potatoes are baking, prepare the coating. In a bowl, mix the flour, garlic powder, paprika, and a pinch of salt and pepper. In another bowl, beat the egg. In a third bowl, place the breadcrumbs. Once the potatoes are done, remove them from the oven and let them cool for a few minutes.
4. Dip each potato stick first in the flour mixture, then the egg, and finally the breadcrumbs, making sure they are evenly coated. Arrange the coated potato sticks back on the baking tray. Sprinkle the grated cheddar cheese evenly over the top of the potatoes.

5. Return the tray to the oven and bake for another 5-10 minutes, until the cheese is melted and bubbly, and the potatoes are golden and crispy.
6. Serve hot with your favourite dipping sauce.

Nutritional Information (per serving)

- Calories: 280 kcal
- Total Fat: 14g
- Saturated Fat: 6g
- Carbohydrates: 34g
- Protein: 6g
- Fiber: 4g
- Sugar: 2g
- Salt: 500mg

Cream Cheese Garlic Bread Bites

Prep Time: 10 minutes   **Cook Time:** 15 minutes   **Servings:** 4

Ingredients

- **1 loaf of French baguette or ciabatta, sliced into 1-inch pieces**
- **200g cream cheese, softened**
- **50g butter, softened**
- **3 cloves garlic, minced**
- **1 tablespoon fresh parsley, chopped**
- **1/2 teaspoon dried oregano**
- **1/2 teaspoon salt**
- **1/4 teaspoon black pepper**
- **50g grated mozzarella cheese (optional)**

Instructions

1. Preheat your oven to 200°C (180°C fan) or 400°F. Line a baking sheet with parchment paper.
2. In a medium bowl, mix the softened cream cheese, butter, minced garlic, chopped parsley, oregano, salt, and black pepper until well combined.
3. Place the sliced bread pieces on the prepared baking sheet. Spread a generous amount of the cream cheese mixture on each slice of bread.
4. If you prefer extra cheesiness, sprinkle a little mozzarella cheese on top of each bite.
5. Bake in the preheated oven for 12-15 minutes, or until the bread is golden and crispy and the cream cheese is bubbly and slightly browned.
6. Remove from the oven and let cool for a minute before serving.
7. Serve these delicious, creamy garlic bread bites warm as a perfect side dish or snack.

Nutritional Information (per serving)

- Calories: 280 kcal
- Total Fat: 18g
- Saturated Fat: 9g
- Carbohydrates: 23g
- Protein: 6g
- Fiber: 1g
- Sugar: 2g
- Salt: 800mg

TikTok Pickle Wraps

Prep Time: 10 minutes   **Cook Time:** 0 minutes   **Servings:** 4

Ingredients

- **4 large flour tortillas**
- **200g cream cheese, softened**
- **1 tablespoon ranch seasoning mix**
- **1 tablespoon Dijon mustard**
- **4 large dill pickles**
- **1 cup deli ham or turkey slices (optional)**
- **Fresh chives, chopped (optional)**

Instructions

1. Spread a thin layer of cream cheese evenly over each tortilla. Sprinkle the ranch seasoning mix across the cream cheese, then drizzle with Dijon mustard. If using, layer a few slices of deli ham or turkey on top of the cream cheese mixture. Place a dill pickle at the edge of each tortilla and roll tightly. Slice the rolled tortillas into bite-sized pieces, arranging them neatly on a plate. Garnish with fresh chives if desired. Serve immediately or refrigerate until ready to enjoy.

Nutritional Information (per serving)

- Calories: 180 kcal
- Total Fat: 12g
- Saturated Fat: 6g
- Carbohydrates: 11g
- Protein: 6g
- Fiber: 1g
- Sugar: 3g
- Salt: 500mg

Hot Honey Chicken Skewers

Prep Time: 15 minutes   **Cook Time:** 10 minutes   **Servings:** 4

Ingredients

- **500g chicken breast, cut into bite-sized cubes**
- **2 tablespoons olive oil**
- **1 tablespoon soy sauce**
- **1 tablespoon garlic, minced**
- **1 tablespoon fresh lemon juice**
- **1 teaspoon smoked paprika**
- **Salt and pepper, to taste**
- **3 tablespoons honey**
- **1 tablespoon sriracha sauce (adjust to heat preference)**
- **1 teaspoon apple cider vinegar**
- **Fresh parsley, chopped (for garnish)**

Instructions

1. First, in a bowl, combine the olive oil, soy sauce, minced garlic, lemon juice, smoked paprika, salt, and pepper. Add the chicken cubes and toss to coat evenly. Allow the chicken to marinate for 10 minutes.
2. While the chicken marinates, preheat your grill or griddle pan over medium-high heat. Thread the marinated chicken onto skewers. Grill the skewers for about 5-7 minutes on each side, or until the chicken is cooked through and lightly charred.
3. While the chicken is cooking, prepare the hot honey sauce. In a small saucepan, combine the honey, sriracha sauce, and apple cider vinegar. Heat over low heat, stirring constantly until the sauce is warm and slightly thickened, about 2-3 minutes. Once the chicken skewers are cooked, drizzle the hot honey sauce over the chicken, ensuring each piece is well coated. Garnish with fresh parsley and serve immediately.

Nutritional Information (per serving)

- Calories: 275 kcal
- Total Fat: 10g
- Saturated Fat: 1.5g
- Carbohydrates: 18g
- Protein: 28g
- Fiber: 0g
- Sugar: 15g
- Salt: 450mg

Cheese Stuffed Onion Rings

Prep Time: 15 minutes   **Cook Time:** 15 minutes   **Servings:** 4

Ingredients

- **2 large onions**
- **100g cheddar cheese, grated**
- **100g cream cheese**
- **1 cup plain flour**
- **1 tsp garlic powder**
- **1 tsp paprika**
- **1/2 tsp salt**
- **1/2 tsp black pepper**
- **2 large eggs, beaten**
- **1 cup breadcrumbs**
- **Vegetable oil for frying**

Instructions

1. To make the onion rings, start by peeling the onions and cutting them into thick slices. Carefully separate the rings, leaving the larger ones intact for stuffing. In a bowl, mix together the grated cheddar cheese and cream cheese until well combined. Stuff the larger onion rings with the cheese mixture, pressing the filling in firmly.
2. In three separate bowls, prepare your dredging stations. In the first bowl, combine the plain flour, garlic powder, paprika, salt, and black pepper. In the second bowl, place the beaten eggs. In the third bowl, add the breadcrumbs. Coat each stuffed onion ring first in the seasoned flour, then dip into the egg, and finally coat in the breadcrumbs.
3. Heat vegetable oil in a deep frying pan or fryer to 180°C (350°F). Fry the coated onion rings in batches for about 3-4 minutes, or until golden brown and crispy. Once done, place the onion rings on a paper towel-lined plate to drain excess oil.

4. Serve the cheese-stuffed onion rings immediately with your favourite dipping sauce.

Nutritional Information (per serving)

- Calories: 320 kcal
- Total Fat: 22g
- Saturated Fat: 9g
- Carbohydrates: 28g
- Protein: 7g
- Fiber: 2g
- Sugar: 5g
- Salt: 500mg

Spinach Dip Puff Pastries

Prep Time: 15 minutes   **Cook Time:** 25 minutes   **Servings:** 4-6

Ingredients

- **1 sheet of puff pastry, thawed**
- **200g fresh spinach, chopped**
- **100g cream cheese, softened**
- **50g grated mozzarella cheese**
- **50g grated Parmesan cheese**
- **1 small garlic clove, minced**
- **1 tablespoon olive oil**
- **Salt and pepper, to taste**
- **1 egg, beaten (for egg wash)**

Instructions

1. Preheat the oven to 200°C (180°C fan) or 400°F. Heat the olive oil in a pan over medium heat and sauté the minced garlic for about 1 minute until fragrant. Add the chopped spinach and cook until wilted, about 3-4 minutes.
2. Remove from the heat and allow to cool slightly. In a mixing bowl, combine the softened cream cheese, mozzarella, Parmesan, sautéed spinach, salt, and pepper. Stir until well combined. Roll out the puff pastry sheet on a lightly floured surface and cut it into 6 equal squares.
3. Place a spoonful of the spinach mixture in the centre of each square. Fold the corners of the pastry over the filling to form a pocket and press the edges to seal. Brush each pastry with the beaten egg to give it a golden finish when baked.
4. Place the filled pastries on a baking tray lined with parchment paper and bake for 20-25 minutes, or until golden and puffed up. Allow to cool slightly before serving.

Nutritional Information (per serving)

- Calories: 230 kcal
- Total Fat: 17g
- Saturated Fat: 8g
- Carbohydrates: 16g
- Protein: 6g
- Fiber: 1g
- Sugar: 1g
- Salt: 350mg

Sweetcorn Fritters

Prep Time: 10 minutes   **Cook Time:** 10 minutes   **Servings:** 4

Ingredients

- 1 can (300g) sweetcorn, drained
- 1 large egg
- 120g plain flour
- 1/2 tsp baking powder
- 1/4 tsp salt
- 1/4 tsp black pepper
- 1/2 tsp paprika
- 1/2 small red onion, finely chopped
- 2 tbsp fresh coriander, chopped
- 2 tbsp milk
- 1 tbsp olive oil (for frying)

Instructions

1. In a large bowl, whisk together the egg, flour, baking powder, salt, pepper, paprika, and milk to form a smooth batter. Add the drained sweet-corn, chopped onion, and fresh coriander to the batter, mixing gently until combined.

2. Heat the olive oil in a non-stick frying pan over medium heat. Once hot, spoon a heaping tablespoon of the batter into the pan for each fritter, flattening them gently with the back of the spoon to form small rounds. Cook for about 2-3 minutes on each side until golden brown and crisp.

3. Once cooked, transfer the fritters to a plate lined with kitchen paper to drain any excess oil. Repeat with the remaining batter, adding more oil if needed.

4. Serve the sweet-corn fritters warm, with a dollop of sour cream or a side of salsa if desired.

Nutritional Information (per serving)

- Calories: 230 kcal
- Total Fat: 10g
- Saturated Fat: 1g
- Carbohydrates: 30g
- Protein: 5g
- Fiber: 3g
- Sugar: 4g
- Salt: 350mg

Baked Zucchini Chips

Prep Time: 10 minutes   **Cook Time:** 20 minutes   **Servings:** 2-3

Ingredients

- 2 medium zucchinis
- 2 tablespoons olive oil
- 1/2 cup breadcrumbs
- (preferably whole wheat)
- 1/4 cup grated Parmesan cheese
- 1 teaspoon garlic powder
- 1/2 teaspoon paprika
- Salt and pepper, to taste

Instructions

1. Preheat your oven to 200°C (180°C fan). Line a baking sheet with parchment paper for easy cleanup. Slice the zucchinis into thin rounds, about 3-5mm thick, ensuring they

are uniform in size for even cooking. In a bowl, toss the zucchini slices with olive oil, ensuring each slice is coated evenly.

2. In a separate shallow dish, mix the breadcrumbs, Parmesan cheese, garlic powder, paprika, salt, and pepper. Dip each zucchini slice into the breadcrumb mixture, pressing gently to coat both sides. Arrange the coated zucchini slices in a single layer on the prepared baking sheet.

3. Bake in the preheated oven for 15-20 minutes or until golden and crispy, flipping the chips halfway through the cooking time for even crispiness. Remove from the oven and serve immediately, with your choice of dipping sauce.

Nutritional Information (per serving)

- Calories: 170 kcal
- Total Fat: 12g
- Saturated Fat: 2g
- Carbohydrates: 14g
- Protein: 5g
- Fiber: 3g
- Sugar: 4g
- Salt: 600mg

Smashed Garlic Potatoes

Prep Time: 10 minutes   **Cook Time:** 30 minutes   **Servings:** 4

Ingredients

- **800g baby new potatoes, washed**
- **3 cloves garlic, minced**
- **2 tablespoons olive oil**
- **1 tablespoon fresh rosemary, chopped**
- **1 teaspoon sea salt**
- **1/2 teaspoon black pepper**
- **1 tablespoon butter**
- **Fresh parsley, for garnish (optional)**

Instructions

1. Start by boiling the baby potatoes in a large pot of salted water for 15-20 minutes, or until they are fork-tender. Drain the potatoes and let them cool for a few minutes.

2. Next, place the potatoes on a baking sheet lined with parchment paper. Use a potato masher or the bottom of a glass to gently smash each potato until flattened but still intact.

3. In a small bowl, mix the minced garlic, olive oil, chopped rosemary, sea salt, and black pepper. Drizzle the garlic mixture over the smashed potatoes, making sure each one is well-coated.

4. Preheat the oven to 200°C (180°C fan)/400°F/gas mark 6. Roast the smashed potatoes in the oven for 20-25 minutes, or until the edges are crispy and golden.

5. Once the potatoes are done, remove them from the oven and sprinkle with a small amount of butter on top of each smashed potato while they're still hot. Garnish with fresh parsley, if desired, and serve immediately.

Nutritional Information (per serving)

- Calories: 210 kcal
- Total Fat: 12g
- Saturated Fat: 2g
- Carbohydrates: 24g
- Protein: 3g
- Fiber: 3g
- Sugar: 2g
- Salt: 750mg

Air-Fryer Chicken Wings

Prep Time: 10 minutes   **Cook Time:** 25 minutes   **Servings:** 4

Ingredients

- **10-12 chicken wings, fresh or frozen**
- **1 tablespoon olive oil**
- **1 teaspoon garlic powder**
- **1 teaspoon onion powder**
- **1 teaspoon smoked paprika**
- **½ teaspoon salt**
- **½ teaspoon black pepper**
- **½ teaspoon dried oregano**
- **2 tablespoons honey (optional for glaze)**
- **Fresh parsley, chopped (for garnish)**

Instructions

1. To begin, pat the chicken wings dry with paper towels to ensure a crispy texture when cooked. In a large bowl, drizzle the olive oil over the chicken wings and toss them to coat evenly. Sprinkle in the garlic powder, onion powder, smoked paprika, salt, pepper, and oregano. Toss again until the wings are evenly coated with the seasoning mix.
2. Preheat the air fryer to 180°C (350°F) for about 5 minutes. Place the seasoned chicken wings in the air fryer basket in a single layer, making sure they aren't overcrowded for even cooking. Cook the wings for 20 minutes, flipping them halfway through to ensure they cook evenly.
3. Once cooked, check the wings to ensure they are crispy and fully cooked. If desired, drizzle honey over the wings and return them to the air fryer for an additional 2-3 minutes for a glossy glaze. Afterward, remove the wings from the air fryer and transfer them to a serving plate. Garnish with freshly chopped parsley before serving.

Nutritional Information (per serving)

- Calories: 250 kcal
- Total Fat: 16g
- Saturated Fat: 3g
- Carbohydrates: 5g
- Protein: 24g
- Fiber: 1g
- Sugar: 3g
- Salt: 600mg

Crispy Parmesan Broccoli Bites

Prep Time: 10 minutes   **Cook Time:** 15 minutes   **Servings:** 4

Ingredients

- **500g broccoli florets**
- **50g grated Parmesan cheese**
- **1/2 cup breadcrumbs (preferably panko)**
- **1 egg, beaten**
- **2 tablespoons olive oil**
- **1 teaspoon garlic powder**
- **1/2 teaspoon onion powder**
- **Salt and pepper to taste**
- **1 tablespoon chopped fresh parsley (optional)**

Instructions

1. Preheat the oven to 200°C (fan oven 180°C) or 400°F. Line a baking tray with parchment paper or a non-stick baking mat.
2. In a large bowl, combine the grated Parmesan cheese, breadcrumbs, garlic powder, onion powder, salt, and pepper. Mix well to ensure everything is evenly distributed.
3. In a separate bowl, beat the egg. Dip each broccoli floret into the beaten egg, making sure it's fully coated, then roll it in the Parmesan breadcrumb mixture until well covered. Repeat with all the florets.
4. Place the coated broccoli florets in a single layer on the prepared baking tray. Drizzle them lightly with olive oil.
5. Bake in the preheated oven for 12-15 minutes or until the broccoli is tender and the breadcrumbs are golden and crispy.
6. Once cooked, remove from the oven and sprinkle with fresh parsley, if desired. Serve immediately as a snack or side dish.

Nutritional Information (per serving)

- Calories: 190 kcal
- Total Fat: 13g
- Saturated Fat: 3g
- Carbohydrates: 13g
- Protein: 7g
- Fiber: 4g
- Sugar: 2g
- Salt: 300mg

TikTok Wonton Crackers

Prep Time: 10 minutes   **Cook Time:** 5 minutes   **Servings:** 4

Ingredients

- 12 wonton wrappers
- 1 tbsp sesame oil
- 1 tbsp soy sauce
- 1 tsp garlic powder
- 1 tsp onion powder
- 1 tsp chili flakes (optional)
- Salt, to taste

- 1 tbsp sesame   seeds (optional)

Instructions

1. Preheat the oven to 180°C (160°C fan)/350°F. Cut each wonton wrapper into triangles by slicing them diagonally. Lay the wonton triangles out in a single layer on a baking tray. In a small bowl, mix together the sesame oil, soy sauce, garlic powder, onion powder, chili flakes (if using), and a pinch of salt.
2. Brush the wonton triangles with the seasoned oil mixture using a pastry brush, making sure both sides are lightly coated. Sprinkle sesame seeds over the top for extra crunch.
3. Bake the wonton crackers in the preheated oven for 4-5 minutes, or until golden brown and crispy. Keep an eye on them as they can burn quickly.
4. Once baked, remove from the oven and let them cool slightly before serving. Serve as a snack or with your favourite dip.

Nutritional Information (per serving)

- Calories: 120 kcal
- Total Fat: 7g
- Saturated Fat: 1g
- Carbohydrates: 13g

- Protein: 2g
- Fiber: 1g
- Sugar: 0g
- Salt: 500mg

Viral Avocado Fries

Prep Time: 10 minutes   **Cook Time:** 15 minutes   **Servings:** 2-3

Ingredients

- **2 ripe avocados**
- **1/2 cup plain flour**
- **2 large eggs, beaten**
- **1 cup breadcrumbs (preferably panko)**

- **1/4 cup grated Parmesan cheese**
- **1 teaspoon garlic powder**
- **1 teaspoon paprika**

- **Salt and pepper, to taste**
- **Olive oil or cooking spray for greasing**

Instructions

1. First, preheat your oven to 200°C (180°C fan) or 400°F. Line a baking tray with parchment paper or lightly grease it with cooking spray.
2. Cut the avocados in half and remove the pits. Carefully scoop the flesh out with a spoon and slice the avocado into 1-inch thick strips.
3. In a shallow bowl, place the plain flour. In another bowl, beat the eggs. In a third bowl, combine the breadcrumbs, Parmesan cheese, garlic powder, paprika, salt, and pepper.

4. Dip each avocado slice into the flour, coating it lightly, then into the beaten eggs, and finally into the breadcrumb mixture, pressing down gently to ensure the breadcrumbs stick.
5. Place the coated avocado fries onto the prepared baking tray in a single layer. Lightly spray them with olive oil to help them crisp up.
6. Bake the avocado fries for 12-15 minutes, flipping halfway through, until golden and crispy on the outside.
7. Serve immediately with a dipping sauce of your choice, such as ranch or sriracha mayo.

Nutritional Information (per serving)
- Calories: 220 kcal
- Total Fat: 16g
- Saturated Fat: 3g
- Carbohydrates: 20g
- Protein: 5g
- Fiber: 8g
- Sugar: 1g
- Salt: 300mg

Pizza Scrolls with a Kick

Prep Time: 15 minutes   **Cook Time:** 20 minutes   **Servings:** 4

Ingredients
- **1 sheet of ready-rolled puff pastry**
- **100g tomato pizza sauce**
- **100g mozzarella cheese, grated**
- **50g pepperoni slices**
- **1/2 teaspoon dried chili flakes**
- **1/2 teaspoon garlic powder**
- **1 tablespoon olive oil**
- **Fresh basil leaves (optional, for garnish)**

Instructions
1. Roll out the puff pastry on a flat surface. Spread the tomato pizza sauce evenly over the entire sheet, leaving a small border around the edges. Sprinkle the mozzarella cheese over the sauce, ensuring it's evenly distributed. Layer the pepperoni slices over the cheese, followed by a generous sprinkling of chili flakes and garlic powder for a spicy kick.
2. Starting from one edge, carefully roll the pastry sheet into a tight log. Slice the rolled pastry into 6-8 equal pieces and place them on a baking tray lined with parchment paper. Brush the top of each scroll with olive oil for a golden, crispy finish.
3. Bake in a preheated oven at 200°C (180°C fan) / 400°F / Gas Mark 6 for 20 minutes or until the scrolls are golden and the cheese is bubbling. Remove from the oven and allow to cool slightly before serving. Garnish with fresh basil leaves if desired.

Nutritional Information (per serving)
- Calories: 300 kcal
- Total Fat: 22g
- Saturated Fat: 8g

- Carbohydrates: 22g
- Protein: 10g
- Fiber: 1g
- Sugar: 3g
- Salt: 600mg

Bang Bang Cauliflower

Prep Time: 15 minutes   **Cook Time:** 20 minutes   **Servings:** 4

Ingredients

- **1 medium cauliflower, cut into florets**
- **2 tbsp olive oil**
- **½ tsp smoked paprika**
- **½ tsp garlic powder**
- **½ tsp salt**
- **¼ tsp black pepper**
- **100g breadcrumbs (preferably panko)**
- **2 tbsp cornflour (cornstarch)**
- **200ml buttermilk or milk (for dipping)**

For the Bang Bang Sauce:

- **3 tbsp mayonnaise**
- **2 tbsp sweet chili sauce**
- **1 tbsp sriracha sauce (or more for extra spice)**
- **1 tsp rice vinegar**
- **1 tsp honey (optional for sweetness)**

Instructions

1. Preheat the oven to 200°C (180°C fan)/400°F. In a large bowl, toss the cauliflower florets with olive oil, smoked paprika, garlic powder, salt, and pepper until evenly coated. In a shallow dish, combine the breadcrumbs and cornflour. Dip each cauliflower floret into the buttermilk, then dredge in the breadcrumb mixture, pressing down lightly to coat well.
2. Place the coated cauliflower florets on a baking sheet lined with parchment paper in a single layer. Bake in the preheated oven for 20 minutes, turning halfway through, until golden and crispy.
3. While the cauliflower is baking, make the bang bang sauce by whisking together the mayonnaise, sweet chili sauce, sriracha sauce, rice vinegar, and honey (if using) in a small bowl.
4. Once the cauliflower is cooked, transfer it to a large mixing bowl. Pour the bang bang sauce over the cauliflower and gently toss to coat evenly. Serve immediately, garnished with fresh coriander or green onions, if desired.

Nutritional Information (per serving)

- Calories: 250 kcal
- Total Fat: 12g
- Saturated Fat: 2g
- Carbohydrates: 31g
- Protein: 5g
- Fiber: 4g
- Sugar: 7g
- Salt: 800mg

Pesto Garlic Knots

Prep Time: 15 minutes   **Cook Time:** 15 minutes   **Servings:** 12 knots

Ingredients

- 1 pack (about 500g) of pizza dough
- 3 tbsp pesto (store-bought or homemade)
- 3 cloves garlic, minced
- 2 tbsp unsalted butter, melted
- 1 tbsp olive oil
- 50g grated Parmesan cheese
- Fresh basil leaves for garnish (optional)
- Salt, to taste

Instructions

1. Preheat your oven to 200°C (180°C fan) or 400°F. Roll the pizza dough out on a lightly floured surface into a rectangle about 1 cm thick. Using a sharp knife or pizza cutter, slice the dough into 12 strips. Twist each strip into a knot shape and place them on a baking tray lined with parchment paper.
2. In a small bowl, mix the melted butter, olive oil, minced garlic, and pesto together. Brush this mixture generously over each garlic knot, making sure each knot is well coated. Sprinkle with Parmesan cheese and a pinch of salt.
3. Bake the knots in the preheated oven for about 12-15 minutes, or until golden and crispy. Remove from the oven and let them cool slightly. Garnish with fresh basil leaves for added flavour (optional).
4. Serve warm and enjoy the perfect bite of garlic, pesto, and cheese in each knot!

Nutritional Information (per serving)

- Calories: 140 kcal
- Total Fat: 8g
- Saturated Fat: 3.5g
- Carbohydrates: 14g
- Protein: 4g
- Fiber: 0.5g
- Sugar: 1g
- Salt: 450mg

BBQ Loaded Sweet Potato Skins

Prep Time: 10 minutes   **Cook Time:** 30 minutes   **Servings:** 4

Ingredients

- 4 medium sweet potatoes
- 200g cooked chicken, shredded
- 100g BBQ sauce (store-bought or homemade)
- 100g cheddar cheese, grated
- 50g spring onions, finely chopped
- 100g sour cream
- 1 tsp smoked paprika

- **1 tsp olive oil**
- **Salt and pepper to taste**
- **Fresh coriander or parsley (optional, for garnish)**

Instructions

1. Start by preheating the oven to 200°C (180°C fan) or 400°F. Scrub the sweet potatoes under cold water and dry them thoroughly. Pierce each sweet potato several times with a fork. Place them on a baking sheet and bake for 25-30 minutes, or until they are soft and tender when pierced with a fork.

2. Once the sweet potatoes are cooked, remove them from the oven and let them cool slightly. When cool enough to handle, slice them in half lengthwise and scoop out most of the flesh, leaving a small border around the edges to form the skins. Keep the flesh for another recipe, like mashed sweet potatoes or a filling.

3. Brush the sweet potato skins with olive oil and season with salt, pepper, and smoked paprika. Place the skins back on the baking sheet and return them to the oven for an additional 10-12 minutes, until the edges are crispy.

4. While the skins are crisping, combine the shredded chicken with BBQ sauce in a bowl. Once the skins are ready, remove them from the oven and spoon the BBQ chicken mixture into each skin. Sprinkle the grated cheese on top and return the skins to the oven for another 5 minutes, or until the cheese has melted and is bubbly.

5. Once the cheese is melted, remove the sweet potato skins from the oven. Top with chopped spring onions, a dollop of sour cream, and fresh coriander or parsley for garnish. Serve immediately.

Nutritional Information (per serving)

- Calories: 350 kcal
- Total Fat: 14g
- Saturated Fat: 7g
- Carbohydrates: 41g
- Protein: 17g
- Fiber: 6g
- Sugar: 12g
- Salt: 600mg

Sriracha Tuna Cakes

Prep Time: 15 minutes   **Cook Time:** 10 minutes   **Servings:** 4

Ingredients

- **2 cans of tuna in spring water (drained, 160g each)**
- **1/4 cup breadcrumbs**
- **(preferably whole wheat)**
- **1 large egg**
- **2 tablespoons mayonnaise**
- **1 tablespoon sriracha sauce (adjust to taste)**
- **1 teaspoon Dijon mustard**
- **1/2 teaspoon garlic powder**

- 1/2 teaspoon onion powder
- 1/2 teaspoon smoked paprika
- Salt and pepper to taste
- 1 tablespoon olive oil (for frying)
- Fresh coriander (optional, for garnish)

Instructions

1. In a large bowl, combine the drained tuna, breadcrumbs, egg, mayonnaise, sriracha sauce, Dijon mustard, garlic powder, onion powder, smoked paprika, salt, and pepper. Mix well until all ingredients are evenly combined and the mixture holds together. Shape the mixture into 8 small patties.
2. Heat the olive oil in a frying pan over medium heat. Once hot, add the tuna cakes to the pan and cook for 3-4 minutes on each side, or until golden brown and crispy. Once cooked, transfer the cakes to a paper towel-lined plate to drain any excess oil.
3. Garnish with fresh coriander if desired and serve immediately.

Nutritional Information (per serving)

- Calories: 240 kcal
- Total Fat: 14g
- Saturated Fat: 2g
- Carbohydrates: 7g
- Protein: 27g
- Fiber: 1g
- Sugar: 1g
- Salt: 350mg

Hummus Stuffed Cucumbers

Prep Time: 10 minutes   **Cook Time:** 0 minutes   **Servings:** 4

Ingredients

- 2 large cucumbers
- 200g hummus (store-bought or homemade)
- 1 tablespoon olive oil
- 1 teaspoon smoked paprika
- Fresh parsley, finely chopped (for garnish)
- Salt and pepper, to taste

Instructions

1. Start by washing the cucumbers thoroughly. Cut off the ends and slice them into 1-inch thick rounds. Use a melon baller or small spoon to scoop out the centre of each cucumber slice, creating a hollow space for the hummus.
2. Take the hummus and fill each cucumber round with a generous spoonful. Drizzle olive oil over the top of the stuffed cucumbers, then sprinkle with smoked paprika for a touch of flavour and colour. Season with salt and pepper to taste.
3. Finally, garnish with freshly chopped parsley for a burst of colour and freshness. Serve immediately as a snack or light appetizer.

Nutritional Information (per serving)

- Calories: 120 kcal
- Total Fat: 8g
- Saturated Fat: 1g

- Carbohydrates: 10g
- Protein: 3g
- Fiber: 2g
- Sugar: 3g
- Salt: 300mg

TikTok Pepperoni Roses

Prep Time: 10 minutes   **Cook Time:** 10 minutes   **Servings:** 4

Ingredients

- **16 slices of pepperoni**
- **2 sheets of puff pastry (ready-rolled)**
- **1/2 cup (about 50g) grated mozzarella cheese**
- **1/4 cup (about 30g) grated parmesan cheese**
- **1 egg (for egg wash)**
- **1 tablespoon tomato sauce (optional)**
- **1/2 teaspoon dried oregano (optional)**

Instructions

1. Preheat the oven to 200°C (180°C fan) or 400°F. Line a baking tray with parchment paper.
2. Roll out the puff pastry on a lightly floured surface and cut each sheet into 4 strips, about 2 inches wide.
3. Place 4 slices of pepperoni on each strip of puff pastry, overlapping them slightly. You want the pepperoni slices to cover about two-thirds of the pastry.
4. Sprinkle a little mozzarella cheese and parmesan cheese on top of the pepperoni slices.
5. Starting at one end of the strip, carefully roll the pastry and pepperoni up into a rose shape. The edges of the pastry should form a spiral around the pepperoni.
6. Place each pepperoni rose on the baking tray, ensuring they are slightly spaced apart.
7. Beat the egg and brush it over the tops of the pepperoni roses to create a golden finish when baked.
8. If desired, drizzle a small amount of tomato sauce over each rose and sprinkle with dried oregano.
9. Bake the roses in the preheated oven for 10 minutes, or until the pastry is golden and puffed and the cheese has melted.

Nutritional Information (per serving)

- Calories: 270 kcal
- Total Fat: 20g
- Saturated Fat: 9g
- Carbohydrates: 17g
- Protein: 10g
- Fiber: 1g
- Sugar: 1g
- Salt: 600mg

Buffalo Cauliflower Wings

Prep Time: 15 minutes   **Cook Time:** 25 minutes   **Servings:** 4

Ingredients

- **1 medium cauliflower, cut into florets**
- **100g plain flour**
- **100ml water**
- **1 teaspoon garlic powder**
- **1 teaspoon paprika**
- **Salt and pepper, to taste**
- **2 tablespoons olive oil**
- **120ml buffalo hot sauce**
- **1 tablespoon melted butter**
- **Fresh parsley (for garnish, optional)**
- **Blue cheese dressing (for serving, optional)**

Instructions

1. Preheat your oven to 200°C (fan 180°C) or 400°F. In a large bowl, whisk together the flour, water, garlic powder, paprika, salt, and pepper to form a smooth batter. Toss the cauliflower florets in the batter, ensuring each piece is evenly coated.
2. Place a baking sheet lined with parchment paper and arrange the battered cauliflower florets in a single layer. Drizzle the olive oil over the florets and bake for 20-25 minutes, flipping halfway through, until golden brown and crispy.
3. While the cauliflower is baking, mix the buffalo hot sauce and melted butter together in a small bowl. Once the cauliflower is done, remove it from the oven and transfer the florets into a clean bowl. Pour the buffalo sauce mixture over the cauliflower and toss to coat each piece.
4. Return the cauliflower to the baking sheet and bake for an additional 5-7 minutes to set the sauce.
5. Remove from the oven, garnish with fresh parsley if desired, and serve with blue cheese dressing on the side.

Nutritional Information (per serving)

- Calories: 180 kcal
- Total Fat: 9g
- Saturated Fat: 2g
- Carbohydrates: 22g
- Protein: 5g
- Fiber: 4g
- Sugar: 4g
- Salt: 350mg

Baked Falafel Balls

Prep Time: 15 minutes   **Cook Time:** 25 minutes   **Servings:** 4

Ingredients

- 1 can (400g) chickpeas, drained and rinsed
- 1 small onion, finely chopped
- 2 garlic cloves, minced
- 1 cup fresh parsley, chopped
- 1/2 cup fresh coriander, chopped
- 1 teaspoon ground cumin
- 1 teaspoon ground coriander
- 1/2 teaspoon ground turmeric
- 1/4 teaspoon ground cinnamon (optional)
- 1 tablespoon tahini
- 2 tablespoons olive oil
- 1 tablespoon lemon juice
- 2-3 tablespoons flour (plain or chickpea flour)
- Salt and pepper, to taste

Instructions

1. In a food processor, combine the chickpeas, onion, garlic, parsley, coriander, cumin, ground coriander, turmeric, cinnamon (if using), tahini, olive oil, and lemon juice. Blend until smooth, stopping to scrape down the sides as needed.
2. Once the mixture is well combined, add flour a tablespoon at a time until the mixture holds together when shaped into balls. Season with salt and pepper to taste.
3. Preheat the oven to 200°C (180°C fan)/400°F. Line a baking tray with parchment paper.
4. Shape the falafel mixture into 12-16 small balls, about the size of a walnut, and place them on the prepared baking tray. Drizzle or spray with a little olive oil.
5. Bake for 20-25 minutes, turning halfway through, until golden and crispy on the outside.
6. Serve with pita bread, a drizzle of tahini, or a side of hummus and salad.

Nutritional Information (per serving)

- Calories: 200 kcal
- Total Fat: 9g
- Saturated Fat: 1g
- Carbohydrates: 25g
- Protein: 7g
- Fiber: 6g
- Sugar: 3g
- Salt: 300mg

Ranch Seasoned Popcorn

Prep Time: 5 minutes   **Cook Time:** 5 minutes   **Servings:** 4

Ingredients

- 100g popcorn kernels
- 2 tablespoons olive oil or melted butter
- 1 packet (about 30g) ranch seasoning mix

- 1/4 teaspoon garlic powder
- 1/4 teaspoon onion powder
- Salt to taste (optional)

Instructions

1. Start by heating a large pot over medium heat. Add the olive oil or melted butter and let it warm up. Once the oil is hot, add the popcorn kernels to the pot. Cover the pot with a lid, leaving a small gap for steam to escape. Shake the pot occasionally to ensure even popping. When the popping slows down, remove the pot from the heat.
2. Transfer the freshly popped popcorn into a large mixing bowl. While the popcorn is still warm, sprinkle the ranch seasoning mix, garlic powder, and onion powder over the top. Toss the popcorn well to coat all the kernels evenly with the seasoning. Taste and add salt if desired.
3. Serve immediately for the best crunch and flavor.

Nutritional Information (per serving)

- Calories: 180 kcal
- Carbohydrates: 22g
- Sugar: 0g
- Total Fat: 9g
- Protein: 3g
- Salt: 300mg
- Saturated Fat: 1g
- Fiber: 3g

Crispy Halloumi Sticks

Prep Time: 10 minutes   **Cook Time:** 5 minutes   **Servings:** 2

Ingredients

- **250g Halloumi cheese, cut into 1 cm thick sticks**
- **2 tbsp plain flour**
- **1 large egg, beaten**
- **50g breadcrumbs (preferably panko for extra crunch)**
- **1 tbsp olive oil or sunflower oil for frying**
- **Fresh lemon wedges, to serve**
- **Fresh parsley (optional), for garnish**
- **Salt and pepper, to taste**

Instructions

1. To start, cut the Halloumi into 1 cm thick sticks. Place the flour in a shallow bowl and season with salt and pepper. In another shallow bowl, beat the egg. In a third bowl, add the breadcrumbs.
2. Dredge each Halloumi stick first in the flour, ensuring it's coated lightly, then dip it into the beaten egg, and finally coat it in the breadcrumbs, pressing gently to ensure the breadcrumbs stick well.
3. Heat the olive oil in a frying pan over medium heat. Once hot, add the Halloumi sticks and fry for 2-3 minutes on each side, until golden brown and crispy.

4. Remove from the pan and place the crispy Halloumi sticks on a plate lined with paper towels to absorb any excess oil.
5. Serve immediately with fresh lemon wedges on the side and a sprinkle of parsley for extra colour.

Nutritional Information (per serving)

- Calories: 320 kcal
- Total Fat: 22g
- Saturated Fat: 12g
- Carbohydrates: 16g
- Protein: 18g
- Fiber: 1g
- Sugar: 2g
- Salt: 1300mg

Honey Butter Corn Ribs

Prep Time: 10 minutes   **Cook Time:** 25 minutes   **Servings:** 4

Ingredients

- **4 ears of corn**
- **50g unsalted butter, melted**
- **2 tbsp honey**
- **1 tsp garlic powder**
- **1 tsp smoked paprika**
- **1/2 tsp salt**
- **1/4 tsp black pepper**
- **Fresh chopped parsley (optional, for garnish)**

Instructions

1. Start by preheating your oven to 200°C (180°C fan) or 400°F. Slice the corn cobs into "ribs" by cutting each ear of corn into 4-5 sections, making sure the knife goes through the cob evenly. Arrange the corn ribs on a baking sheet lined with parchment paper.
2. In a small bowl, mix the melted butter, honey, garlic powder, smoked paprika, salt, and pepper. Brush the mixture generously over the corn ribs, ensuring each piece is well coated. Reserve a little bit of the honey butter for brushing the corn later.
3. Bake the corn ribs in the preheated oven for 20-25 minutes, flipping halfway through, until they are golden and slightly crispy on the edges.
4. Once the corn is cooked, remove from the oven and brush with the remaining honey butter. Garnish with freshly chopped parsley for an added touch of freshness.
5. Serve hot as a delicious side dish or snack.

Nutritional Information (per serving)

- Calories: 180 kcal
- Total Fat: 10g
- Saturated Fat: 6g
- Carbohydrates: 24g
- Protein: 2g
- Fiber: 3g
- Sugar: 9g
- Salt: 350mg

TikTok Pizza Bread Bowl

Prep Time: 10 minutes   **Cook Time:** 15 minutes   **Servings:** 2

Ingredients

- **2 large round sourdough or ciabatta rolls (for the bowls)**
- **200g pizza sauce**
- **150g mozzarella cheese, shredded**
- **50g pepperoni slices (optional)**
- **1/2 teaspoon dried oregano**
- **1/2 teaspoon garlic powder**
- **Fresh basil leaves for garnish**
- **Olive oil for brushing**

Instructions

1. Start by preheating your oven to 200°C (180°C fan)/400°F/gas mark 6. Cut the tops off the rolls and hollow out the insides, leaving a 1.5 cm border around the edge to form a bowl. Set the hollowed-out bread aside.
2. Brush the inside of each bread bowl lightly with olive oil and place them on a baking sheet. Spoon the pizza sauce evenly into each bread bowl, filling them about halfway. Sprinkle a layer of mozzarella cheese over the sauce, then add pepperoni slices if using. Sprinkle oregano and garlic powder on top of the cheese for added flavour.
3. Place the bread bowls in the oven and bake for about 10-12 minutes, or until the cheese is melted and bubbly, and the bread is slightly toasted.
4. Once out of the oven, garnish with fresh basil leaves for a burst of flavour.
5. Serve immediately while hot and enjoy this deliciously cheesy TikTok-inspired pizza bread bowl!

Nutritional Information (per serving)

- Calories: 520 kcal
- Total Fat: 22g
- Saturated Fat: 8g
- Carbohydrates: 58g
- Protein: 18g
- Fiber: 3g
- Sugar: 6g
- Salt: 700mg

Loaded Nacho Fries

Prep Time: 10 minutes   **Cook Time:** 20 minutes   **Servings:** 4

Ingredients

- **500g frozen fries (or homemade fries)**
- **200g grated cheddar cheese**
- **100g cooked chicken (shredded) or beef mince**
- **1 small red onion, finely chopped**
- **1 small tomato, diced**
- **1/2 cup sour cream**

- 2 tbsp guacamole
- 1 jalapeño, sliced (optional)
- 1 tbsp olive oil
- 1 tsp smoked paprika
- 1 tsp garlic powder
- 1/2 tsp ground cumin
- Salt and pepper, to taste
- Fresh coriander (cilantro), chopped, for garnish

Instructions

1. Preheat your oven to 200°C (180°C fan) or 400°F. Spread the frozen fries in a single layer on a baking tray, drizzle with olive oil, and season with smoked paprika, garlic powder, cumin, salt, and pepper. Bake for 20 minutes or until golden and crispy, turning them halfway through.
2. While the fries are baking, cook your choice of meat. If using chicken, heat a pan over medium heat, add the chicken, and cook until browned. Season with a pinch of salt and pepper. If using beef mince, cook in a pan over medium heat until browned, draining any excess fat.
3. Once the fries are done, remove them from the oven and sprinkle with half of the grated cheddar cheese. Return them to the oven for 2-3 minutes to melt the cheese. Afterward, top with the cooked chicken or beef, chopped red onion, diced tomato, and the remaining cheese. Bake for another 2-3 minutes until the cheese is fully melted.
4. Remove the loaded fries from the oven and garnish with jalapeño slices, a dollop of sour cream, guacamole, and fresh coriander. Serve immediately.

Nutritional Information (per serving)

- Calories: 420 kcal
- Total Fat: 22g
- Saturated Fat: 8g
- Carbohydrates: 38g
- Protein: 18g
- Fiber: 4g
- Sugar: 3g
- Salt: 900mg

Viral Desserts

Dalgona Whipped Coffee

Prep Time: 5 minutes   **Cook Time:** 0 minutes   **Servings:** 1

Ingredients

- 2 tablespoons instant coffee granules
- 2 tablespoons granulated sugar
- 2 tablespoons hot water
- 200ml milk (dairy or plant-based)
- Ice cubes (optional, for iced coffee)

Instructions

1. Combine instant coffee, sugar, and hot water in a medium-sized bowl. Use a hand whisk, electric mixer, or frother to whip the mixture vigorously until it becomes thick and creamy, with stiff peaks forming. This process usually takes 2-5 minutes depending on the tool used.
2. If serving iced, fill a glass with ice cubes. Pour milk over the ice or directly into a mug if serving warm. Spoon the whipped coffee mixture on top of the milk, creating a layered effect. Gently stir the whipped coffee into the milk before drinking for the best flavour.

Nutritional Information (per serving)

- Calories: 150 kcal
- Total Fat: 5g (depends on milk choice)
- Saturated Fat: 3g
- Carbohydrates: 25g
- Protein: 6g
- Fiber: 0g
- Sugar: 22g
- Salt: 0.2g

Oreo Mug Cake Explosion

Prep Time: 5 minutes   **Cook Time:** 2 minutes   **Servings:** 1

Ingredients

- 4 Oreo cookies
- 4 tablespoons of milk (whole or semi-skimmed)
- 2 tablespoons of plain flour
- ½ teaspoon of baking powder
- 1 tablespoon of sugar (optional, for extra sweetness)
- 1 tablespoon of chocolate chips (optional)
- A dollop of whipped cream or a scoop of vanilla

ice cream for   topping

Instructions

1. Place the Oreo cookies in a large microwave-safe mug and crush them into small pieces using a fork.
2. Add the milk to the mug and stir until the cookies are soft and form a paste-like consistency. Stir in the plain flour, baking powder, and sugar (if using) until fully combined, ensuring no lumps remain.
3. If desired, mix in the chocolate chips for an extra chocolatey explosion. Microwave the mug on high power for 1-2 minutes, checking after 1 minute to prevent overcooking.
4. The cake is done when it rises and appears set in the centre. Allow the mug cake to cool slightly before topping it with whipped cream or a scoop of vanilla ice cream. Serve warm and enjoy!

Nutritional Information (per serving)

- Calories: 290 kcal
- Total Fat: 11g
- Saturated Fat: 4g
- Carbohydrates: 40g
- Protein: 5g
- Fiber: 1g
- Sugar: 25g
- Salt: 170mg

Galaxy Swirl Cheesecake

Prep Time: 20 minutes   **Cook Time:** 1 hour   **Servings:** 12

Ingredients

For the Base:
- 250g digestive biscuits, crushed
- 100g unsalted butter, melted

For the Cheesecake Filling:

- 500g cream cheese, softened
- 200g caster sugar
- 200ml double cream
- 3 large eggs
- 1 tsp vanilla extract

Food colouring:

blue, purple, pink, and black

For the Swirl Effect:
- Edible glitter (optional)
- 50g white chocolate, melted

Instructions

1. Prepare the base by combining the crushed digestive biscuits and melted butter in a bowl until the mixture resembles wet sand. Press it firmly into the bottom of a 20cm springform cake tin and refrigerate while preparing the filling.
2. In a large mixing bowl, beat the cream cheese and caster sugar until smooth and creamy. Add the eggs one at a time, mixing well after each addition. Pour in the double cream and vanilla extract, then mix until fully combined. Divide the mixture evenly into four bowls and colour each portion with blue, purple, pink, and black food colouring.

3. Remove the biscuit base from the fridge and pour the coloured mixtures alternately into the tin to create layers. Use a skewer or the back of a spoon to swirl the colours gently for a galaxy effect. Avoid over-mixing to maintain distinct colours.
4. Bake the cheesecake in a preheated oven at 160°C (fan 140°C) for 55-60 minutes, or until the edges are set and the centre has a slight wobble. Turn off the oven and leave the cheesecake inside with the door slightly ajar to cool gradually. Once cooled, refrigerate for at least 6 hours or overnight.
5. Before serving, drizzle the melted white chocolate over the top in a random pattern and sprinkle with edible glitter for a galaxy sparkle. Slice and enjoy your cosmic creation.

Nutritional Information (per serving)
- Calories: 380 kcal
- Total Fat: 24g
- Saturated Fat: 14g
- Carbohydrates: 31g
- Protein: 6g
- Fiber: 1g
- Sugar: 21g
- Salt: 0.4g

TikTok Cookie Dough Balls

Prep Time: 15 minutes   **Cook Time:** 0 minutes   **Servings:** 12 balls

Ingredients
- **125g plain flour (heat-treated for safety)**
- **100g unsalted butter, softened**
- **75g light brown sugar**
- **50g caster sugar**
- **1 tsp vanilla extract**
- **2 tbsp milk**
- **100g chocolate chips (milk, dark, or white)**
- **Pinch of salt**

Instructions
1. To make the flour safe for raw consumption, spread it evenly on a baking tray and bake at 180°C for 5 minutes, then allow it to cool completely.
2. Cream together the softened butter, light brown sugar, and caster sugar in a large mixing bowl until light and fluffy. Mix in the vanilla extract, milk, and a pinch of salt until fully combined.
3. Gradually fold in the cooled, heat-treated flour, mixing until the dough comes together. Stir in the chocolate chips to evenly distribute them throughout the dough.
4. Use a small cookie scoop or your hands to roll the dough into 12 bite-sized balls. Place the balls on a tray or plate lined with baking paper and chill in the fridge for at least 15 minutes before serving.

Nutritional Information (per ball)
- Calories: 120 kcal
- Total Fat: 6g
- Saturated Fat: 3.5g
- Carbohydrates: 15g
- Protein: 1g
- Fiber: 0.5g

- Sugar: 10g
- Salt: 50mg

Caramelised Sugar Churros

Prep Time: 15 minutes   **Cook Time:** 20 minutes   **Servings:** 4

Ingredients
- **1 cup (250ml) water**
- **2 tablespoons unsalted butter**
- **2 tablespoons granulated sugar**
- **1/4 teaspoon salt**
- **1 cup (120g) plain flour**
- **2 large eggs**
- **1 teaspoon vanilla extract**
- **Oil for frying (vegetable or sunflower oil)**
- **1/2 cup (100g) granulated sugar (for coating)**
- **1 teaspoon ground cinnamon (optional)**

Instructions
1. In a medium saucepan, combine the water, butter, sugar, and salt. Heat over medium heat until the mixture comes to a boil and the butter has melted. Remove the saucepan from the heat and add the flour all at once, stirring vigorously until a dough forms and pulls away from the sides of the pan. Allow the dough to cool slightly for 5 minutes.
2. Once the dough has cooled, beat in the eggs one at a time, mixing well after each addition. Add the vanilla extract and mix until the dough is smooth and glossy. Transfer the dough to a piping bag fitted with a star nozzle.
3. In a deep frying pan or large pot, heat the oil to 175°C (350°F). Pipe 10-12cm (4-5 inch) lengths of dough directly into the hot oil, using scissors to cut the dough as you go. Fry the churros in batches, turning occasionally, until golden brown and crispy, about 3-4 minutes per batch. Remove the churros with a slotted spoon and drain on paper towels.
4. In a shallow bowl, mix the granulated sugar with the cinnamon (if using). Roll the warm churros in the sugar mixture until coated evenly. Serve immediately with your favourite dipping sauce, such as melted chocolate or dulce de leche.

Nutritional Information (per serving)
- Calories: 250 kcal
- Total Fat: 11g
- Saturated Fat: 3g
- Carbohydrates: 33g
- Protein: 4g
- Fiber: 1g
- Sugar: 15g
- Salt: 150mg

Rainbow Fruit Jelly Cups

Prep Time: 20 minutes   **Cook Time:** 10 minutes   **Servings:** 6

Ingredients

- 1 packet (135g) of strawberry jelly (or any red jelly flavour)
- 1 packet (135g) of orange jelly
- 1 packet (135g) of lime jelly
- 1 cup of blueberries
- 1 cup of diced kiwi
- 1 cup of diced mango
- 1 cup of diced strawberries
- 1 cup of whipped cream (optional, for topping)
- 6 clear cups or dessert glasses

Instructions

1. Prepare the strawberry jelly as per the packet instructions, typically dissolving the jelly crystals in boiling water and then adding cold water. Pour a thin layer of the jelly into each of the clear cups, dividing it evenly, and place a few pieces of diced strawberries into each. Allow this layer to set in the fridge for 20-30 minutes.
2. While the first layer sets, prepare the orange jelly using the same method. Once the red jelly layer is firm, carefully pour the orange jelly over it, dividing it evenly between the cups. Add a layer of diced mango to each cup and return them to the fridge to set.
3. Repeat the process with the lime jelly. Once the orange layer has set, pour the lime jelly evenly into the cups, and top each with diced kiwi and a few blueberries. Place the cups back in the fridge to set completely, which may take another 2-3 hours.
4. Before serving, optionally top each jelly cup with a dollop of whipped cream for extra indulgence.

Nutritional Information (per serving)

- Calories: 150 kcal
- Total Fat: 0.5g
- Saturated Fat: 0.2g
- Carbohydrates: 36g
- Protein: 2g
- Fiber: 2g
- Sugar: 29g
- Salt: 90mg

2-Ingredient Nutella Mousse

Prep Time: 10 minutes   **Cook Time:** 0 minutes   **Servings:** 4

Ingredients

- 250ml double cream (cold)
- 150g Nutella

Instructions

1. Chill a mixing bowl in the refrigerator for 10-15 minutes to ensure the cream whips easily. Once chilled, pour the double cream into the bowl and whip it using an electric mixer on medium speed until soft peaks form. This process should take about 2-3 minutes.
2. Gently warm the Nutella in the microwave for 10-15 seconds to loosen its consistency, making it easier to fold into the whipped cream. Let it cool slightly if necessary to prevent melting the cream.
3. Add the Nutella to the whipped cream in small increments, folding gently with a spatula to combine. Take care not to overmix, as this can deflate the mousse.
4. Divide the mousse into serving glasses or bowls, smoothing the tops with a spoon or spatula. Cover the glasses with cling film and refrigerate for at least 2 hours to allow the mousse to set.
5. Before serving, optionally garnish with a dollop of whipped cream, chocolate shavings, or chopped hazelnuts.

Nutritional Information (per serving)

- Calories: 340 kcal
- Total Fat: 28g
- Saturated Fat: 15g
- Carbohydrates: 22g
- Protein: 3g
- Fiber: 1g
- Sugar: 20g
- Salt: 30mg

Mini Donut Cereal

Prep Time: 20 minutes   **Cook Time:** 10 minutes   **Servings:** 4

Ingredients

- **200g plain flour**
- **50g caster sugar**
- **1 tsp baking powder**
- **¼ tsp salt**
- **1 large egg**
- **120ml whole milk**
- **2 tbsp unsalted butter, melted**
- **1 tsp vanilla extract**
- **Oil for frying**
- **50g icing sugar (for glaze)**
- **1 tbsp milk (for glaze)**
- **Sprinkles (optional)**

Instructions

1. In a large bowl, mix together the flour, caster sugar, baking powder, and salt. In a separate bowl, whisk the egg, milk, melted butter, and vanilla extract until well combined. Gradually add the wet ingredients to the dry ingredients, stirring until a smooth dough forms.
2. Transfer the dough to a piping bag fitted with a small round nozzle. Pipe tiny circles onto a sheet of parchment paper, creating mini donut shapes. Heat oil in a deep pan to 180°C and carefully drop in the mini donuts in small batches. Fry for 1-2 minutes on

each side until golden brown, then transfer to a plate lined with kitchen paper to drain excess oil.

3. For the glaze, mix the icing sugar and milk in a small bowl until smooth. Dip each mini donut into the glaze, then place on a wire rack to set. Add sprinkles on top for extra fun if desired. Serve in a bowl with milk for the full cereal effect.

Nutritional Information (per serving)

- Calories: 310 kcal
- Total Fat: 12g
- Saturated Fat: 5g
- Carbohydrates: 45g
- Protein: 5g
- Fiber: 1g
- Sugar: 20g
- Salt: 150mg

Layered Chocolate Dream Bar

Prep Time: 20 minutes (plus chilling time)   **Cook Time:** 10 minutes   **Servings:** 12

Ingredients

- **200g digestive biscuits, crushed**
- **100g unsalted butter, melted**
- **150g milk chocolate, chopped**
- **150g dark chocolate, chopped**
- **150ml double cream**
- **100g white chocolate, chopped**
- **50ml double cream (for white chocolate layer)**
- **Optional toppings: crushed nuts, sprinkles, or grated chocolate**

Instructions

1. Combine the crushed digestive biscuits and melted butter in a mixing bowl, stirring until the mixture resembles wet sand. Press the mixture firmly into the base of a lined 20cm square baking tin to create an even layer. Place the tin in the fridge to set for 15 minutes.

2. Melt the milk and dark chocolate together in a heatproof bowl over simmering water, ensuring the bowl does not touch the water. Once smooth, remove from the heat and stir in 150ml of double cream until well combined. Pour this mixture over the chilled biscuit base, spreading it evenly. Refrigerate for 1 hour until set.

3. Melt the white chocolate in a separate bowl using the same method. Once smooth, stir in 50ml of double cream until the mixture is silky. Pour the white chocolate layer over the set dark chocolate layer, spreading evenly. Sprinkle with your chosen toppings if desired.

4. Return the tin to the fridge and chill for at least 2 hours, or until completely set. Once firm, slice into 12 bars and serve.

Nutritional Information (per serving)

- Calories: 310 kcal
- Total Fat: 22g
- Saturated Fat: 13g
- Carbohydrates: 24g
- Protein: 3g
- Fiber: 1g
- Sugar: 19g
- Salt: 0.2g

TikTok Brownie Cookies

Prep Time: 15 minutes   **Cook Time:** 12 minutes   **Servings:** 12 cookies

Ingredients
- **200g dark chocolate (around 70% cocoa), chopped**
- **100g unsalted butter**
- **2 large eggs**
- **150g granulated sugar**
- **50g brown sugar**
- **1 tsp vanilla extract**
- **125g plain flour**
- **2 tbsp cocoa powder**
- **1/2 tsp baking powder**
- **1/4 tsp salt**
- **100g chocolate chips or chunks**

Instructions
1. Melt the dark chocolate and butter together in a heatproof bowl over simmering water or in short bursts in the microwave. Stir until smooth, then set aside to cool for a few minutes. In a separate bowl, whisk together the eggs, granulated sugar, brown sugar, and vanilla extract until light and fluffy.
2. Add the melted chocolate mixture to the egg mixture and stir until fully combined. In another bowl, sift the plain flour, cocoa powder, baking powder, and salt together. Gradually fold the dry ingredients into the wet mixture until just combined, being careful not to overmix.
3. Stir in the chocolate chips or chunks. Preheat your oven to 180°C (160°C fan) and line a baking tray with parchment paper. Drop tablespoon-sized portions of dough onto the tray, spacing them about 2 inches apart. Bake for 10-12 minutes, until the edges are set but the centre is still soft.
4. Allow the cookies to cool on the tray for 5 minutes before transferring them to a wire rack to cool completely.

Nutritional Information (per cookie)
- Calories: 210 kcal
- Total Fat: 13g
- Saturated Fat: 8g
- Carbohydrates: 23g
- Protein: 2g
- Fiber: 2g
- Sugar: 18g
- Salt: 70mg

Cotton Candy Ice Cream Sandwich

Prep Time: 15 minutes   **Cook Time:** 0 minutes   **Servings:** 4

Ingredients

- **4 large cookies (store-bought or homemade, preferably soft and chewy)**
- **2 cups cotton candy ice cream**
- **(or vanilla ice cream mixed with cotton candy flavouring)**
- **1/4 cup mini marshmallows**
- **1/4 cup rainbow sprinkles**
- **1 tbsp powdered sugar (optional, for dusting)**

Instructions

1. Start by placing the cookies on a flat surface. If you're using store-bought cookies, ensure they are soft and chewy for the best texture. If you prefer homemade, let them cool completely before assembling the sandwiches.
2. Scoop the cotton candy ice cream onto the flat side of two cookies. Use about 1/2 cup of ice cream per sandwich. Spread it evenly with the back of a spoon, making sure to cover the entire surface.
3. Top the ice cream with mini marshmallows and rainbow sprinkles. Press the second cookie gently on top, creating a sandwich with the ice cream in the middle.
4. If desired, lightly dust the outer edges of the sandwich with powdered sugar for an extra sweet touch. Repeat this process for the remaining cookies and ice cream.
5. Once assembled, place the ice cream sandwiches in the freezer for at least 30 minutes to firm up. This will help the sandwiches hold their shape and prevent the ice cream from melting too quickly when serving.
6. Serve chilled and enjoy your cotton candy ice cream sandwiches!

Nutritional Information (per serving)

- Calories: 450 kcal
- Total Fat: 20g
- Saturated Fat: 8g
- Carbohydrates: 62g
- Protein: 4g
- Fiber: 2g
- Sugar: 40g
- Salt: 200mg

Stuffed Cookie Ice Cream Cones

Prep Time: 20 minutes   **Cook Time:** 12 minutes   **Servings:** 6

Ingredients

- **6 ice cream cones (waffle cones)**
- **150g unsalted butter, softened**
- **100g white sugar**
- **100g brown sugar**

- 1 large egg
- 1 tsp vanilla extract
- 200g plain flour
- 1/2 tsp baking soda
- 1/4 tsp salt
- 100g milk chocolate chips
- 100g mini marshmallows
- 200g vanilla ice cream (or your preferred flavour)

Instructions

1. Preheat your oven to 180°C (160°C fan) and line a baking sheet with parchment paper. In a large bowl, cream together the softened butter, white sugar, and brown sugar until light and fluffy. Add the egg and vanilla extract, and mix until well combined.

2. In a separate bowl, whisk together the flour, baking soda, and salt. Gradually add the dry ingredients to the wet ingredients, mixing until a dough forms. Stir in the chocolate chips and mini marshmallows.

3. Spoon a small amount of dough into the bottom of each ice cream cone, pressing it down slightly. Add a small scoop of ice cream on top of the dough, then place more cookie dough around the ice cream to fill the cone completely. You can gently press the dough around the sides of the ice cream to hold it in place.

4. Place the stuffed cones upright on the prepared baking sheet, and bake for 10-12 minutes, or until the cookie dough is golden brown and cooked through. Allow the cones to cool for a few minutes before serving.

5. Serve the stuffed cookie ice cream cones as a fun dessert treat, and enjoy!

Nutritional Information (per serving)

- Calories: 450 kcal
- Total Fat: 23g
- Saturated Fat: 12g
- Carbohydrates: 58g
- Protein: 4g
- Fiber: 2g
- Sugar: 35g
- Salt: 210mg

Matcha Cream Puffs

Prep Time: 30 minutes   **Cook Time:** 25 minutes   **Servings:** 12 puffs

Ingredients

For the Choux Pastry:
- 75g unsalted butter
- 150ml water
- 1 tsp caster sugar
- 1/2 tsp salt
- 100g plain flour

- 3 large eggs
- 1 tsp vanilla extract

For the Matcha Cream Filling:
- 200ml double cream
- 2 tbsp icing sugar

- 1 1/2 tsp matcha powder
- 1/2 tsp vanilla extract

Instructions

1. To make the choux pastry, first, preheat the oven to 200°C (180°C fan) or 400°F. Line a baking tray with parchment paper. In a saucepan, combine the butter, water, sugar, and salt. Place the saucepan over medium heat and bring it to a simmer until the butter has melted completely. Remove the pan from the heat and immediately stir in the flour. Mix until a dough forms, then return the pan to low heat and cook for 2-3 minutes to dry out the dough slightly.

2. Remove the dough from the pan and allow it to cool for a few minutes. Once slightly cooled, add the eggs one at a time, stirring after each addition until the dough becomes smooth and glossy. Stir in the vanilla extract. Transfer the dough to a piping bag and pipe small, round mounds (about 3cm in diameter) onto the prepared baking tray, leaving space between each puff.

3. Bake in the preheated oven for 20-25 minutes, or until golden brown and puffed. Turn off the oven and leave the puffs inside for an additional 5 minutes to dry out. Remove from the oven and set aside to cool completely.

4. To make the matcha cream filling, place the double cream, icing sugar, and matcha powder in a mixing bowl. Whisk until the cream forms soft peaks. Stir in the vanilla extract. Transfer the cream to a piping bag fitted with a small round nozzle.

5. Once the puffs have cooled, carefully make a small hole at the bottom of each puff. Pipe the matcha cream into the centre of each puff, filling them generously. Serve immediately or refrigerate until ready to enjoy.

Nutritional Information (per serving)

- Calories: 180 kcal
- Total Fat: 12g
- Saturated Fat: 7g
- Carbohydrates: 16g
- Protein: 2g
- Fiber: 0g
- Sugar: 6g
- Salt: 0.1g

Sticky Toffee Pudding Cake

Prep Time: 15 minutes   **Cook Time:** 45 minutes   **Servings:** 8

Ingredients

For the cake:
- **200g pitted dates, chopped**
- **300ml boiling water**
- **1 tsp baking soda**
- **50g unsalted butter, softened**
- **100g dark brown sugar**
- **2 large eggs**
- **200g self-raising flour**
- **1 tsp vanilla extract**
- **1/2 tsp ground cinnamon**
- **Pinch of salt**

For the toffee sauce:
- **200g soft brown sugar**
- **100g unsalted butter**
- **200ml double cream**
- **1 tbsp golden syrup**
- **Pinch of sea salt**

Instructions

1. To begin, place the chopped dates in a bowl and pour over the boiling water. Stir in the baking soda, and let the mixture sit for about 10 minutes to soften the dates.
2. In a separate bowl, cream the softened butter and dark brown sugar together until light and fluffy. Add the eggs one at a time, beating well after each addition. Mix in the vanilla extract.
3. Next, sift the flour, cinnamon, and salt into the bowl with the butter and sugar mixture. Gradually fold in the flour mixture, then pour in the date mixture, including the liquid, and stir gently to combine.
4. Transfer the batter into a greased 8-inch (20 cm) baking dish and spread it evenly. Bake at 180°C (160°C fan) / 350°F / Gas Mark 4 for 40-45 minutes or until the cake is risen and a skewer inserted into the centre comes out clean.
5. While the cake is baking, make the toffee sauce. In a saucepan, melt the butter over medium heat, then stir in the brown sugar, golden syrup, and double cream. Bring to a simmer, stirring constantly, and cook for about 3-4 minutes until the sauce thickens. Add a pinch of sea salt and remove from the heat.
6. Once the cake is baked, remove it from the oven and allow it to cool for a few minutes. Poke holes all over the top of the cake with a skewer or fork, and then pour over half of the toffee sauce, allowing it to soak into the cake.
7. Serve slices of the sticky toffee pudding warm, drizzled with the remaining toffee sauce. Optionally, serve with vanilla ice cream or custard for extra indulgence.

Nutritional Information (per serving)

- Calories: 410 kcal
- Total Fat: 22g
- Saturated Fat: 12g
- Carbohydrates: 51g
- Sugar: 45g
- Protein: 3g
- Fiber: 2g
- Salt: 0.3g

TikTok Honeycomb Candy

Prep Time: 10 minutes   **Cook Time:** 10 minutes   **Servings:** 12 pieces

Ingredients

- **200g caster sugar**
- **5 tbsp golden syrup**
- **1 tsp bicarbonate of soda**
- **1 tbsp butter**
- **A pinch of sea salt (optional)**

Instructions

1. Start by lining a baking tray with parchment paper or a silicone mat to prevent sticking. In a medium-sized saucepan, combine the caster sugar and golden syrup. Place the saucepan over medium heat and stir occasionally until the sugar has fully dissolved. Once dissolved, stop stirring and bring the mixture to a boil. Let it bubble for

around 4-5 minutes, or until it reaches a deep amber colour. It is important to keep an eye on it, as it can burn quickly once it starts to change colour.

2. Once the mixture has reached the correct colour, remove the saucepan from the heat. Immediately stir in the bicarbonate of soda; the mixture will bubble up rapidly. Stir quickly to incorporate the soda into the syrup. Add the butter and sea salt (if using), then give it another quick stir.

3. Quickly pour the bubbly mixture into the prepared baking tray. Let the candy set and cool for about 30 minutes, or until firm. Once cooled, break it into chunks by tapping the tray or using your hands. Enjoy your homemade TikTok honeycomb candy!

Nutritional Information (per serving)

- Calories: 160 kcal
- Total Fat: 1g
- Saturated Fat: 0.5g
- Carbohydrates: 38g
- Sugars: 37g
- Protein: 0g
- Fiber: 0g
- Salt: 0.1g

Lemon Drizzle Gooey Bars

Prep Time: 15 minutes   **Cook Time:** 25 minutes   **Servings:** 12

Ingredients
For the Bars:
- **200g unsalted butter, softened**
- **150g caster sugar**
- **2 large eggs**
- **200g self-raising flour**

- **1 tsp baking powder**
- **Zest of 1 lemon**
- **1 tbsp lemon juice**
- **100g white chocolate chips (optional)**

For the Lemon Drizzle:
- **100g icing sugar**
- **2 tbsp lemon juice**
- **Zest of 1 lemon**

Instructions

1. To make the bars, preheat the oven to 180°C (160°C fan)/350°F/ Gas Mark 4. Grease and line a 9x9-inch square baking tin.

2. In a large mixing bowl, cream together the softened butter and caster sugar until light and fluffy. Beat in the eggs one at a time, adding a little flour with each egg to prevent curdling. Mix in the lemon zest and lemon juice.

3. Sift the self-raising flour and baking powder together, then fold them into the wet ingredients until well combined. If using, gently stir in the white chocolate chips.

4. Pour the batter into the prepared tin and smooth it out evenly. Bake in the preheated oven for 20-25 minutes, or until the top is golden and a skewer inserted into the center comes out with only a few moist crumbs. The middle should still be slightly gooey.

5. While the bars are baking, make the lemon drizzle. In a small bowl, combine the icing sugar, lemon juice, and lemon zest. Stir until smooth and runny.

6. Once the bars are out of the oven, allow them to cool in the tin for about 10 minutes. While still slightly warm, drizzle the lemon mixture over the bars. Let them cool completely before slicing into squares.

Nutritional Information (per serving)

- Calories: 250 kcal
- Total Fat: 13g
- Saturated Fat: 8g
- Carbohydrates: 32g
- Protein: 2g
- Fiber: 0.5g
- Sugar: 20g
- Salt: 0.3g

TikTok Peanut Butter Blossoms

Prep Time: 15 minutes   **Cook Time:** 10 minutes   **Servings:** 12 cookies

Ingredients

- **150g peanut butter (smooth or crunchy)**
- **100g caster sugar**
- **100g light brown sugar**
- **1 large egg**
- **1 teaspoon vanilla extract**
- **180g plain flour**
- **1/2 teaspoon baking soda**
- **1/4 teaspoon salt**
- **12 milk chocolate or dark chocolate Kisses (or similar chocolate sweets)**
- **Extra sugar for rolling**

Instructions

1. Start by preheating the oven to 180°C (160°C fan) or 350°F and line a baking tray with parchment paper. In a mixing bowl, combine the peanut butter, caster sugar, and light brown sugar. Use an electric mixer or whisk to cream them together until smooth. Beat in the egg and vanilla extract until fully combined.

2. In a separate bowl, whisk the plain flour, baking soda, and salt together. Gradually add the dry ingredients to the wet mixture, stirring until a dough forms. Shape the dough into small balls, about 1 inch (2.5 cm) in diameter. Roll each ball in extra sugar before placing them on the prepared baking tray, spacing them about 2 inches apart.

3. Bake the cookies in the preheated oven for 8-10 minutes, until the edges are golden and the centres are set. Remove the tray from the oven and gently press a chocolate kiss into the centre of each cookie while still warm. Allow the cookies to cool on the tray for a few minutes before transferring them to a wire rack to cool completely.

Nutritional Information (per cookie)

- Calories: 180 kcal
- Total Fat: 11g
- Saturated Fat: 3g
- Carbohydrates: 20g
- Protein: 3g
- Fiber: 1g
- Sugar: 15g
- Salt: 100mg

TikTok Cinnamon Roll Dumplings

Prep Time: 10 minutes   **Cook Time:** 20 minutes   **Servings:** 4

Ingredients

- **1 can (375g) of ready-made cinnamon roll dough**
- **50g unsalted butter, melted**
- **3 tablespoons brown sugar**
- **1 teaspoon ground cinnamon**
- **1/2 cup (120ml) water**
- **1/2 cup (120ml) milk**
- **100g cream cheese, softened**
- **2 tablespoons icing sugar**
- **1 teaspoon vanilla extract**

Instructions

1. To make the cinnamon rolls, preheat the oven to 180°C (160°C fan) or 350°F. Open the can of cinnamon roll dough and separate the rolls. Cut each roll into quarters to make small dumpling-sized pieces. In a mixing bowl, combine the melted butter, brown sugar, and cinnamon. Toss the cinnamon roll pieces in the mixture, ensuring they are fully coated.

2. Transfer the coated dough pieces into a greased oven-safe baking dish. In a separate bowl, whisk together the water and milk, then pour this mixture over the dough pieces. Bake in the preheated oven for about 20 minutes, or until the dumplings are golden and cooked through.

3. While the dumplings are baking, make the icing by mixing the softened cream cheese, icing sugar, and vanilla extract together in a small bowl. Once the dumplings are done, drizzle the cream cheese icing over the warm cinnamon roll dumplings and serve immediately.

Nutritional Information (per serving)

- Calories: 380 kcal
- Total Fat: 22g
- Saturated Fat: 12g
- Carbohydrates: 40g
- Protein: 4g
- Fiber: 1g
- Sugar: 22g
- Salt: 200mg

TikTok Cookie Dough Milkshake

Prep Time: 10 minutes   **Cook Time:** 0 minutes   **Servings:** 2

Ingredients

- **4 scoops vanilla ice cream**
- **1 cup whole milk**
- **2 tablespoons cookie dough (safe-to-eat, or use edible cookie dough)**
- **2 teaspoons chocolate chips**
- **1 tablespoon peanut butter (optional)**
- **Whipped cream, for topping**
- **Mini chocolate chips, for garnish**
- **1 teaspoon vanilla extract (optional)**

Instructions

1. In a blender, combine the vanilla ice cream, whole milk, cookie dough, chocolate chips, and peanut butter (if using). Blend until smooth and creamy.
2. If you prefer a thicker consistency, add more ice cream; if you'd like it thinner, add a bit more milk. Once blended, pour the milkshake into two glasses.
3. Top with whipped cream, mini chocolate chips, and a drizzle of additional cookie dough or chocolate syrup. Serve immediately with a straw and enjoy!

Nutritional Information (per serving)

- Calories: 450 kcal
- Total Fat: 28g
- Saturated Fat: 14g
- Carbohydrates: 50g
- Sugar: 45g
- Protein: 6g
- Fiber: 1g
- Salt: 140mg

TikTok Fried Ice Cream

Prep Time: 15 minutes   **Cook Time:** 2 minutes   **Servings:** 4

Ingredients

- 4 scoops vanilla ice cream
- 1 cup cornflakes, crushed
- ½ cup desiccated coconut
- 2 tbsp brown sugar
- 1 tsp cinnamon
- 1 egg, beaten
- 1 cup plain flour
- Vegetable oil (for frying)
- Honey or chocolate sauce (for serving, optional)

Instructions

1. Start by scooping the ice cream into 4 equal portions. Roll each scoop into a ball using your hands or a spoon. Place the ice cream balls on a tray lined with parchment paper and freeze for at least 1 hour to firm up.
2. Next, prepare the coating by crushing the cornflakes into small pieces. In a bowl, mix the crushed cornflakes, desiccated coconut, brown sugar, and cinnamon. In a separate bowl, place the flour, and in another bowl, beat the egg.
3. Once the ice cream balls are firm, dip each one first into the flour, ensuring it's fully coated. Then, dip it into the beaten egg, followed by rolling it in the cornflake mixture,

pressing gently to coat evenly. Return the coated ice cream balls to the freezer for another 30 minutes to ensure they stay firm during frying.

4. While the ice cream balls are freezing, heat vegetable oil in a deep frying pan or pot over medium heat. The oil should be hot but not smoking. Carefully fry the ice cream balls for about 2 minutes, turning them to ensure an even golden crust. Remove from the oil and place on paper towels to drain excess oil.

5. Serve immediately, drizzling with honey or chocolate sauce if desired.

Nutritional Information (per serving)

- Calories: 250 kcal
- Total Fat: 15g
- Saturated Fat: 6g
- Carbohydrates: 28g
- Protein: 3g
- Fiber: 2g
- Sugar: 12g
- Salt: 150mg

UK-INSPIRED TIKTOK RECIPES

Full English Breakfast Toast

Prep Time: 10 minutes   **Cook Time:** 15 minutes   **Servings:** 2

Ingredients
- 2 slices of thick-cut bread
- 2 large eggs
- 2 sausages
- 2 rashers of back bacon
- 1/2 cup baked beans
- 1/2 tomato, sliced
- 2 tbsp butter
- Olive oil, for frying
- Salt and pepper, to taste
- Fresh parsley, for garnish

Instructions
1. Start by frying the sausages and bacon in a pan with a little olive oil over medium heat. Cook the sausages for about 10-12 minutes, turning occasionally, until browned and fully cooked.
2. Fry the bacon for 3-4 minutes on each side, or until crispy. Remove the sausages and bacon from the pan and set them aside. In the same pan, toast the bread slices in a little butter until golden brown and crispy, about 2-3 minutes on each side. Set the toast aside.
3. While the toast is cooking, heat the baked beans in a small pot over low heat until warmed through. In a separate pan, heat some olive oil and fry the eggs to your desired doneness, either sunny-side up or scrambled.
4. Meanwhile, grill or pan-fry the tomato slices for about 2 minutes on each side, until slightly charred. To assemble, place the toast on plates, then top each slice with a fried egg, bacon, sausage, baked beans, grilled tomato, and fresh parsley. Season with salt and pepper to taste and serve immediately.

Nutritional Information (per serving)
- Calories: 700 kcal
- Total Fat: 35g
- Saturated Fat: 12g
- Carbohydrates: 50g
- Protein: 32g
- Fiber: 5g
- Sugar: 8g
- Salt: 1.5g

Yorkshire Pudding Wrap

Prep Time: 10 minutes   **Cook Time:** 25 minutes   **Servings:** 4

Ingredients

- **200g plain flour**
- **4 large eggs**
- **300ml whole milk**
- **1/2 tsp salt**
- **1 tbsp vegetable oil**
- **400g cooked roast beef (or your choice of protein)**
- **2 tbsp horseradish sauce (optional)**
- **100g rocket leaves**
- **1 large onion, sliced**
- **1 tbsp olive oil**
- **2 tbsp balsamic vinegar**
- **Gravy for serving (optional)**

Instructions

1. Preheat your oven to 220°C (200°C fan) or 450°F. In a large bowl, whisk together the flour, eggs, milk, and salt until smooth to form the batter. Set it aside to rest for 10 minutes. Heat the oil in a 12-cup muffin tin or a baking tray in the oven for 5 minutes, ensuring it's hot before pouring in the batter.
2. Carefully remove the tin from the oven and evenly pour the batter into each cup, filling them about halfway. Return the tin to the oven and bake for 20-25 minutes, or until the Yorkshire puddings are puffed up and golden brown. While they cook, prepare the fillings.
3. In a frying pan, heat the olive oil over medium heat and sauté the sliced onion until soft and caramelized, about 10 minutes. Add the balsamic vinegar to the pan to deglaze and cook for another 2 minutes, then remove from heat.
4. Once the Yorkshire puddings are done, remove them from the oven and allow them to cool for a minute. Carefully slice off the tops to open them up like a wrap. To assemble, fill each Yorkshire pudding with a portion of the roast beef, caramelized onions, a drizzle of horseradish sauce (if using), and a handful of rocket leaves. If you like, pour a little gravy over the filling or serve on the side for dipping.

Nutritional Information (per serving)

- Calories: 380 kcal
- Total Fat: 20g
- Saturated Fat: 5g
- Carbohydrates: 30g
- Protein: 20g
- Fiber: 3g
- Sugar: 8g
- Salt: 450mg

Scotch Egg Bites

Prep Time: 15 minutes   **Cook Time:** 20 minutes   **Servings:** 4

Ingredients

- **4 large sausages (preferably sausages with a**
- **good seasoning, like Cumberland)**
- **4 boiled eggs**
- **100g breadcrumbs**
- **50g plain flour**
- **1 large egg (for egg wash)**

- **Salt and pepper to taste**
- **Oil for frying**

Instructions

1. Start by boiling the eggs. Place the eggs in a saucepan of water, bring it to a boil, and simmer for 7-8 minutes. Remove the eggs from the boiling water, cool them under cold water, and peel the shells off once cooled.
2. Next, remove the sausage meat from the sausage casings. Flatten out the sausage meat into thin patties, big enough to wrap around each boiled egg.
3. Season the sausage meat with salt and pepper, then take one boiled egg at a time and wrap the sausage meat around it, making sure it is fully covered.
4. Set up a breading station. In one shallow bowl, place the flour, seasoned with a pinch of salt and pepper. In the second bowl, beat the egg for an egg wash. In the third bowl, place the breadcrumbs.
5. Dip each sausage-wrapped egg first into the flour, then into the egg wash, and finally coat it in the breadcrumbs. Ensure that each egg is thoroughly covered in breadcrumbs.
6. Heat oil in a frying pan over medium heat. Fry the Scotch egg bites in batches, turning occasionally, for 5-7 minutes or until golden brown and crispy on all sides.
7. Once cooked, remove the Scotch egg bites from the pan and drain on a paper towel.
8. Serve immediately while still warm, or allow them to cool slightly before serving as an appetizer.

Nutritional Information (per serving)

- Calories: 380 kcal
- Total Fat: 23g
- Saturated Fat: 7g
- Carbohydrates: 23g
- Protein: 18g
- Fiber: 2g
- Sugar: 1g
- Salt: 800mg

TikTok Shepherd's Pie Dumplings

Prep Time: 15 minutes   **Cook Time:** 25 minutes   **Servings:** 4

Ingredients

- **500g minced lamb (or beef for variation)**
- **1 medium onion, finely chopped**
- **2 cloves garlic, minced**
- **2 medium carrots, diced**
- **1 cup frozen peas**
- **2 tablespoons tomato paste**
- **1 cup beef or vegetable stock**
- **1 tablespoon Worcestershire sauce**
- **1 teaspoon dried thyme**
- **1 teaspoon dried rosemary**
- **500g mashed potatoes (prepared in advance)**

- **1 pack of ready-made dumpling wrappers (about 20 wrappers)**
- **Salt and pepper to taste**
- **Olive oil for cooking**

Instructions

1. In a large frying pan, heat a small amount of olive oil over medium heat. Add the minced lamb and cook until browned, breaking it up with a spoon as it cooks. Once browned, remove any excess fat and add the chopped onion and garlic. Cook for about 3-4 minutes until softened.
2. Add the diced carrots, peas, tomato paste, stock, Worcestershire sauce, thyme, and rosemary. Stir well and simmer for 10-12 minutes, until the mixture thickens slightly. Season with salt and pepper to taste. Set aside to cool.
3. Once the filling has cooled slightly, prepare your dumpling wrappers. Place a spoonful of the shepherd's pie mixture in the centre of each wrapper. Top with a small dollop of mashed potatoes. Gently fold the edges of the wrapper together and seal tightly, pinching the sides to form a dumpling.
4. Bring a large pot of water to a boil and add a pinch of salt. Carefully drop the dumplings into the boiling water, cooking them for about 8-10 minutes, or until they float to the surface and the wrappers are cooked through.
5. Remove the dumplings from the water with a slotted spoon and set them on a plate. You can optionally crisp them up by frying the dumplings in a little olive oil in a pan for 2-3 minutes until golden brown.
6. Serve the shepherd's pie dumplings hot, garnished with fresh herbs if desired.

Nutritional Information (per serving)

- Calories: 400 kcal
- Total Fat: 20g
- Saturated Fat: 7g
- Carbohydrates: 35g
- Protein: 22g
- Fiber: 4g
- Sugar: 6g
- Salt: 800mg

Coronation Chicken Salad Cups

Prep Time: 15 minutes   **Cook Time:** 0 minutes   **Servings:** 4

Ingredients

- **2 cooked chicken breasts, shredded**
- **3 tablespoons mayonnaise**
- **2 tablespoons Greek yogurt**
- **1 tablespoon curry powder**
- **1 tablespoon mango chutney**
- **1 teaspoon lemon juice**
- **1/4 cup raisins or sultanas**
- **1/4 cup toasted almonds, chopped**
- **Salt and pepper to taste**

- 8 small lettuce leaves (such as gem or butterhead lettuce)

Instructions

1. To make the coronation chicken filling, mix together the mayonnaise, Greek yogurt, curry powder, mango chutney, and lemon juice in a bowl. Add the shredded chicken and stir until well combined. Then, fold in the raisins (or sultanas) and chopped almonds. Season with salt and pepper to taste.
2. Carefully arrange the lettuce leaves on a serving platter, creating little cups for the salad. Spoon the coronation chicken mixture evenly into each lettuce cup, filling them generously.
3. Serve the coronation chicken salad cups immediately, or refrigerate them for up to an hour before serving for a chilled option.

Nutritional Information (per serving)

- Calories: 240 kcal
- Total Fat: 16g
- Saturated Fat: 2g
- Carbohydrates: 10g
- Protein: 18g
- Fiber: 2g
- Sugar: 8g
- Salt: 250mg

TikTok Fish and Chips Tacos

Prep Time: 15 minutes   **Cook Time:** 20 minutes   **Servings:** 4

Ingredients

- 4 small white fish fillets (such as cod or haddock)
- 1 cup plain flour
- 1/2 cup cornflour
- 1 tsp baking powder
- 1/2 tsp salt
- 1/2 tsp pepper
- 1/2 tsp smoked paprika
- 1/2 cup cold sparkling water
- 8 small soft tortillas
- 2 medium potatoes, peeled and thinly sliced into fries
- 2 tbsp olive oil
- 1 tbsp fresh parsley, chopped (optional)
- 1 lemon, cut into wedges
- Tartar sauce or aioli, to serve

Instructions

1. To start, preheat the oven to 200ºC (fan) or 220ºC (conventional). Arrange the thinly sliced potatoes on a baking tray, drizzle with olive oil, and season with salt and pepper. Toss the fries to coat them evenly, then spread them in a single layer and bake in the preheated oven for 20 minutes, flipping halfway through, until golden and crispy.

2. Meanwhile, prepare the fish batter. In a bowl, mix together the plain flour, cornflour, baking powder, salt, pepper, and smoked paprika. Gradually add the cold sparkling water to the dry ingredients, whisking until the batter is smooth and slightly thick.

3. Heat a deep pan or frying pan with enough oil to shallow fry the fish. Dip the fish fillets into the batter, coating them fully, and fry for 4-5 minutes on each side, or until golden brown and crispy. Once cooked, remove the fish from the pan and place it on a plate lined with paper towels to drain any excess oil.

4. While the fish is cooking, warm the tortillas in a dry pan for 30 seconds on each side or until soft and warm.

5. Once everything is ready, assemble the tacos. Place two tortillas on each plate, then top with a few pieces of crispy fish. Add a generous handful of baked fries, then drizzle with tartar sauce or aioli. Garnish with fresh parsley and a squeeze of lemon juice, and serve with extra lemon wedges on the side.

Nutritional Information (per serving)

- Calories: 490 kcal
- Total Fat: 22g
- Saturated Fat: 3g
- Carbohydrates: 56g
- Protein: 18g
- Fiber: 5g
- Sugar: 3g
- Salt: 600mg

British Pub Curry Loaded Fries

Prep Time: 15 minutes   **Cook Time:** 25 minutes   **Servings:** 4

Ingredients

- **500g frozen fries**
- **1 tablespoon olive oil**
- **1 medium onion, finely chopped**
- **2 cloves garlic, minced**
- **1 tablespoon curry powder**
- **1 teaspoon ground cumin**
- **1 teaspoon ground turmeric**
- **1/2 teaspoon chili powder (optional)**
- **200ml coconut milk**
- **1 tablespoon tomato paste**
- **100g cooked chicken (optional), shredded**
- **75g cheddar cheese, grated**
- **Fresh coriander, chopped (for garnish)**
- **Salt and pepper, to taste**

Instructions

1. Preheat the oven to 200°C (180°C fan) or 400°F. Spread the frozen fries on a baking sheet in a single layer and bake according to package instructions until golden and crispy, about 20-25 minutes.

2. While the fries are baking, heat olive oil in a frying pan over medium heat. Add the chopped onion and cook until soft and translucent, about 5 minutes. Add the minced

garlic and cook for another minute until fragrant. Stir in the curry powder, cumin, turmeric, and chili powder (if using) and cook for 1-2 minutes, allowing the spices to bloom.

3. Pour in the coconut milk and add the tomato paste. Stir until well combined, then bring to a simmer. Let the sauce cook for 5-7 minutes, stirring occasionally, until it thickens slightly. If you're using cooked chicken, stir it into the sauce and heat through for another 2-3 minutes. Season with salt and pepper to taste.

4. Once the fries are done, remove them from the oven and transfer them to a serving plate. Pour the curry sauce evenly over the fries. Sprinkle with grated cheddar cheese, allowing it to melt from the heat of the sauce. Garnish with freshly chopped coriander before serving.

Nutritional Information (per serving)

- Calories: 460 kcal
- Total Fat: 25g
- Saturated Fat: 9g
- Carbohydrates: 48g
- Protein: 9g
- Fiber: 5g
- Sugar: 4g
- Salt: 700mg

Sticky Toffee Cheesecake

Prep Time: 20 minutes   **Cook Time:** 1 hour   **Chill Time:** 4 hours   **Servings:** 8

Ingredients

For the base:

- **200g digestive biscuits, crushed**
- **100g unsalted butter, melted**
- **1 tbsp brown sugar**

For the cheesecake filling:

- **600g cream cheese, softened**

- **200ml double cream**
- **100g caster sugar**
- **2 large eggs**
- **1 tsp vanilla extract**
- **200g toffee sauce (store-bought or homemade)**

For the toffee topping:

- **100g brown sugar**

- **50g unsalted butter**
- **2 tbsp double cream**
- **A pinch of sea salt**

Instructions

1. To prepare the base, start by mixing the crushed digestive biscuits, melted butter, and brown sugar in a bowl until fully combined. Press this mixture into the base of a springform cake tin, making sure it's evenly distributed. Chill in the fridge while you make the filling.

2. For the cheesecake filling, beat the cream cheese and caster sugar together in a bowl until smooth. Add the eggs, one at a time, beating well after each addition. Stir in the

vanilla extract and toffee sauce until combined. Pour the mixture over the chilled biscuit base and smooth the top with a spatula.

3. Bake in a preheated oven at 160°C (140°C fan) for 50-60 minutes, or until the centre is just set but still slightly wobbly. Allow the cheesecake to cool to room temperature, then refrigerate for at least 4 hours or overnight to fully set.

4. For the toffee topping, place the brown sugar, butter, and double cream in a small saucepan. Heat gently until the butter has melted and the sugar has dissolved. Bring to a simmer for 3-4 minutes, then remove from the heat and stir in the sea salt. Allow the sauce to cool to room temperature before drizzling over the chilled cheesecake.

5. Slic and serve chilled, with extra toffee sauce if desired.

Nutritional Information (per serving)

- Calories: 460 kcal
- Total Fat: 28g
- Saturated Fat: 16g
- Carbohydrates: 48g
- Sugar: 35g
- Protein: 6g
- Fiber: 1g
- Salt: 0.2g

TikTok Shandy Jelly

Prep Time: 15 minutes   **Cook Time:** 5 minutes   **Servings:** 4

Ingredients

- **300ml lemonade**
- **300ml beer (lager or ale, depending on preference)**
- **1 packet (12g) of gelatin powder**
- **2 tbsp sugar (optional, adjust to taste)**
- **1 lemon, thinly sliced (for garnish)**

Instructions

1. Start by pouring the lemonade into a small saucepan. Heat it gently over low to medium heat until it begins to warm, but not boil. Once warm, sprinkle the gelatin powder over the lemonade and whisk until fully dissolved. Add sugar to the mixture, stirring until it's completely dissolved. Remove the saucepan from the heat and allow it to cool for a few minutes.

2. Once cooled, slowly pour in the beer while gently stirring to combine. Make sure the mixture is well combined but avoid stirring too vigorously to preserve the carbonation of the beer. Pour the mixture into a shallow dish or individual serving cups and place it in the fridge to set for about 3-4 hours or until firm.

3. After the jelly has set, garnish with thin slices of lemon and serve chilled.

Nutritional Information (per serving)

- Calories: 120 kcal
- Total Fat: 0g
- Saturated Fat: 0g
- Carbohydrates: 30g
- Sugars: 27g
- Protein: 1g

- Fiber: 0g
- Salt: 4mg

Classic Victoria Sponge Mug Cake

Prep Time: 5 minutes   **Cook Time:** 1 minute   **Servings:** 1

Ingredients
- **3 tbsp self-raising flour**
- **3 tbsp caster sugar**
- **2 tbsp unsalted butter, melted**
- **2 tbsp whole milk**
- **1/2 tsp vanilla extract**
- **1 tbsp strawberry jam**
- **1 tbsp double cream (or whipped cream)**

Instructions
1. In a microwave-safe mug, combine the self-raising flour and caster sugar. Stir in the melted butter, milk, and vanilla extract, mixing well until you have a smooth batter.
2. Microwave the mug on high for 1 minute. Check if the cake is cooked by inserting a toothpick or fork; it should come out clean. If not, microwave for an additional 10-15 seconds. Once cooked, allow the mug cake to cool for a few minutes before carefully spreading the strawberry jam on top. Add a dollop of double cream or whipped cream and enjoy your delicious mini Victoria sponge!

Nutritional Information (per serving)
- Calories: 330 kcal
- Total Fat: 18g
- Saturated Fat: 10g
- Carbohydrates: 38g
- Protein: 3g
- Fiber: 1g
- Sugar: 23g
- Salt: 0.2g

TikTok Beans on Toast Tartlets

Prep Time: 15 minutes   **Cook Time:** 20 minutes   **Servings:** 4

Ingredients
- **1 tin (400g) baked beans**
- **4 small, ready-made shortcrust pastry tartlet cases**
- **1 tablespoon olive oil**
- **1 small onion, finely chopped**
- **1 clove garlic, minced**
- **100g mature cheddar cheese, grated**
- **1 tablespoon Worcestershire sauce**
- **1 teaspoon smoked paprika**
- **Salt and pepper, to taste**

- **Fresh parsley for** garnish (optional)

Instructions

1. Preheat the oven to 180°C (160°C fan) or 350°F. Place the tartlet cases onto a baking tray and set aside.

2. In a frying pan, heat the olive oil over medium heat. Add the chopped onion and garlic and cook for 3-4 minutes, until softened and fragrant. Add the baked beans to the pan and stir in the Worcestershire sauce, smoked paprika, salt, and pepper. Allow the beans to simmer for 5 minutes to heat through and thicken slightly.

3. Spoon the baked bean mixture into each tartlet case, filling them generously. Top with grated cheddar cheese, spreading it evenly over the beans. Place the tartlets in the preheated oven and bake for 10-12 minutes, or until the cheese is melted and bubbly, and the pastry is golden brown.

4. Remove from the oven and garnish with fresh parsley, if desired. Serve immediately.

Nutritional Information (per serving)

- Calories: 290 kcal
- Total Fat: 15g
- Saturated Fat: 7g
- Carbohydrates: 30g
- Protein: 9g
- Fiber: 5g
- Sugar: 5g
- Salt: 550mg

Healthy & Fittok Favourites

Protein Pancake Tacos

Prep Time: 10 minutes   **Cook Time:** 10 minutes   **Servings:** 2

Ingredients

- 1 scoop of vanilla protein powder
- 2 large eggs
- 1/2 cup of milk (dairy or non-dairy)
- 1/2 cup of oats
- 1/2 teaspoon of baking powder
- 1/2 teaspoon of vanilla extract
- 1 tablespoon of honey or maple syrup
- Pinch of salt
- 1 tablespoon of coconut oil or butter for cooking
- Toppings: Fresh fruit, Greek yogurt, peanut butter, or syrup

Instructions

1. First, blend the oats in a food processor or blender until finely ground to create oat flour. Then, in a bowl, whisk together the protein powder, eggs, milk, oat flour, baking powder, vanilla extract, honey, and a pinch of salt until smooth.
2. Heat the coconut oil or butter in a non-stick frying pan over medium heat. Once the pan is hot, pour small amounts of batter into the pan, forming small pancake-sized circles.
3. Cook for 2-3 minutes on each side until golden brown and cooked through. To assemble, fold each pancake into taco-shaped folds and fill with your favorite toppings such as fresh fruit, Greek yogurt, peanut butter, or a drizzle of maple syrup. Serve immediately and enjoy!

Nutritional Information (per serving)

- Calories: 400 kcal
- Total Fat: 18g
- Saturated Fat: 6g
- Carbohydrates: 34g
- Protein: 30g
- Fiber: 5g
- Sugar: 8g
- Salt: 250mg

Baked Veggie Crisps

Prep Time: 15 minutes   **Cook Time:** 25 minutes   **Servings:** 4

Ingredients

- 2 medium sweet potatoes, thinly sliced
- 2 medium carrots, thinly sliced
- 1 courgette (zucchini), thinly sliced
- 1 tablespoon olive oil
- 1 teaspoon paprika
- 1 teaspoon garlic powder
- 1/2 teaspoon sea salt
- Freshly ground black pepper, to taste

Instructions

1. Preheat your oven to 180°C (160°C fan) or 350°F. Line a baking tray with parchment paper. In a large bowl, toss the thinly sliced sweet potatoes, carrots, and courgette with olive oil until evenly coated.
2. Sprinkle over the paprika, garlic powder, sea salt, and freshly ground black pepper. Toss everything together to ensure the vegetables are well-seasoned.
3. Spread the vegetables out in a single layer on the prepared baking tray. Be sure not to overcrowd them, as this will help them crisp up better. Bake in the preheated oven for 20-25 minutes, flipping the crisps halfway through.
4. The veggies should be golden and crispy when done. Remove from the oven and let them cool for a few minutes before serving.

Nutritional Information (per serving)

- Calories: 130 kcal
- Total Fat: 6g
- Saturated Fat: 0.5g
- Carbohydrates: 20g
- Protein: 2g
- Fiber: 5g
- Sugar: 5g
- Salt: 350mg

Low-Cal Cauliflower Pizza Bites

Prep Time: 15 minutes   **Cook Time:** 20 minutes   **Servings:** 4

Ingredients

- 1 medium cauliflower, grated or processed into rice-sized pieces
- 100g mozzarella cheese, grated
- 50g Parmesan cheese, grated
- 1 large egg
- 1 tsp dried oregano
- 1/2 tsp garlic powder
- 1/2 tsp onion powder
- Salt and pepper, to taste
- 2 tbsp tomato sauce (for topping)
- 1/4 cup mini pepperoni (optional)
- Fresh basil leaves, for garnish (optional)

Instructions

1. Preheat your oven to 200ºC (180ºC fan) or 400ºF. Line a baking tray with parchment paper.
2. Grate the cauliflower or pulse it in a food processor until it resembles rice. Place it in a clean kitchen towel or cheesecloth and squeeze out as much moisture as possible.
3. In a large bowl, combine the cauliflower with mozzarella, Parmesan, egg, oregano, garlic powder, onion powder, and season with salt and pepper. Mix everything together until a dough-like consistency forms.
4. Take small spoonfuls of the mixture and shape them into bite-sized discs. Place them on the prepared baking tray, ensuring they are evenly spaced.
5. Bake for 15-20 minutes, or until the cauliflower bites are golden and crispy on the edges.
6. Once out of the oven, spread a small spoonful of tomato sauce on each cauliflower bite. Top with mini pepperoni (if using) and return to the oven for an additional 5 minutes, until the cheese is melted.
7. Remove from the oven and garnish with fresh basil leaves, if desired. Serve warm.

Nutritional Information (per serving)
- Calories: 140 kcal
- Total Fat: 9g
- Saturated Fat: 4g
- Carbohydrates: 6g
- Protein: 12g
- Fiber: 3g
- Sugar: 2g
- Salt: 350mg

Sweet Potato Toast Trio

Prep Time: 10 minutes   **Cook Time:** 15 minutes   **Servings:** 2

Ingredients
- **1 large sweet potato**
- **1 tablespoon olive oil**
- **Salt and pepper, to taste**

Topping 1: Avocado & Cherry Tomato
- **1 ripe avocado, mashed**
- **6 cherry tomatoes, halved**

- **A sprinkle of chilli flakes**

Topping 2: Peanut Butter & Banana
- **2 tablespoons natural peanut butter**
- **1 small banana, sliced**
- **A drizzle of honey**

Topping 3: Greek Yoghurt & Berries

- **3 tablespoons plain Greek yoghurt**
- **A handful of mixed berries (blueberries, raspberries, or strawberries)**
- **A sprinkle of granola**

Instructions

1. Preheat the oven to 200°C (180°C fan) and line a baking tray with parchment paper. Wash and peel the sweet potato, then slice it lengthwise into 1cm-thick slices. Brush both sides of the slices lightly with olive oil and season with salt and pepper. Arrange the slices on the prepared baking tray and bake for 12-15 minutes, flipping halfway through, until tender but firm enough to hold toppings.
2. For the avocado and cherry tomato topping, spread mashed avocado over the sweet potato slice and top with cherry tomato halves. Sprinkle with chilli flakes for a touch of spice.
3. For the peanut butter and banana topping, spread natural peanut butter over the sweet potato slice and arrange banana slices on top. Drizzle with honey for added sweetness.
4. For the Greek yoghurt and berries topping, spoon Greek yoghurt over the sweet potato slice and scatter mixed berries over it. Add a sprinkle of granola for crunch.
5. Serve the sweet potato toasts warm or at room temperature as a colourful, nutritious breakfast or snack.

Nutritional Information (per serving)
- Calories: 280 kcal
- Total Fat: 12g
- Saturated Fat: 2g
- Carbohydrates: 38g
- Protein: 7g
- Fibre: 6g
- Sugar: 14g
- Salt: 150mg

Overnight Oat Parfaits

Prep Time: 10 minutes   **Cook Time:** None   **Servings:** 2

Ingredients
- **1 cup (100g) rolled oats**
- **1 cup (250ml) unsweetened almond milk (or milk of choice)**
- **1 tablespoon chia seeds**
- **1 tablespoon honey or maple syrup (optional)**
- **1/2 teaspoon vanilla extract**
- **1/2 cup (125g) Greek yoghurt**
- **1/2 cup (75g) mixed berries (e.g.,**
- **strawberries, blueberries, raspberries)**
- **2 tablespoons granola (for topping)**
- **Fresh mint leaves (optional, for garnish)**

Instructions
1. In a bowl or container, mix the rolled oats, almond milk, chia seeds, honey, and vanilla extract until well combined. Cover and refrigerate overnight or for at least 6 hours.

2. When ready to assemble, stir the overnight oats to ensure an even consistency. In serving glasses or jars, layer the ingredients starting with a base of overnight oats.
3. Add a layer of Greek yoghurt, followed by a layer of mixed berries. Repeat the layers until the jars are filled, finishing with berries on top.
4. Sprinkle granola on top just before serving to maintain its crunch. Garnish with fresh mint leaves if desired and serve chilled.

Nutritional Information (per serving)
- Calories: 270 kcal
- Total Fat: 6g
- Saturated Fat: 1g
- Carbohydrates: 42g
- Protein: 10g
- Fiber: 6g
- Sugar: 12g
- Salt: 50mg

Spinach Banana Smoothie Bowls

Prep Time: 10 minutes   **Cook Time:** None   **Servings:** 2

Ingredients
- **2 medium bananas, frozen and sliced**
- **1 cup fresh spinach leaves, packed**
- **1 cup unsweetened almond milk (or any preferred milk)**
- **½ cup plain Greek yoghurt**
- **1 tablespoon honey or maple syrup (optional, for sweetness)**
- **1 tablespoon chia seeds (optional)**

For Toppings:
- **Granola**
- **Fresh fruit (e.g., sliced strawberries, blueberries, kiwi)**
- **Shredded coconut**
- **Nuts or seeds**

Instructions
1. In a blender, combine the frozen banana slices, fresh spinach, almond milk, Greek yoghurt, and optional honey or maple syrup. Blend on high until the mixture is smooth and creamy.
2. If the mixture is too thick, add a little more almond milk to achieve the desired consistency. Pour the smoothie mixture into two bowls. Top each bowl with granola, fresh fruit, shredded coconut, and nuts or seeds as desired. Serve immediately.

Nutritional Information (per serving)
- Calories: 250 kcal
- Total Fat: 6g
- Saturated Fat: 2g
- Carbohydrates: 40g
- Protein: 8g
- Fiber: 6g
- Sugar: 23g
- Salt: 90mg

Green Goddess Salad Wraps

Prep Time: 15 minutes   **Cook Time:** 0 minutes   **Servings:** 4

Ingredients

For the Salad Wraps:
- **4 large whole wheat tortilla wraps**
- **1 head of romaine lettuce, chopped**
- **1 cucumber, diced**
- **1 avocado, sliced**
- **150g cherry tomatoes, halved**
- **100g shredded carrots**
- **50g crumbled feta cheese (optional)**

For the Green Goddess Dressing:
- **100g Greek yoghurt**
- **1 small clove of garlic, minced**
- **2 tablespoons olive oil**
- **Juice of 1 lemon**
- **2 tablespoons chopped fresh parsley**
- **2 tablespoons chopped fresh** basil
- 1 tablespoon chopped chives
- Salt and pepper, to taste

Instructions

1. Start by preparing the Green Goddess dressing. In a small bowl, mix the Greek yoghurt, minced garlic, olive oil, lemon juice, parsley, basil, and chives until well combined. Season with salt and pepper to taste, then set aside.
2. Lay out the tortilla wraps on a clean surface. Spread a generous amount of the Green Goddess dressing evenly over each wrap. Layer the romaine lettuce, diced cucumber, sliced avocado, cherry tomatoes, shredded carrots, and crumbled feta (if using) down the center of each wrap.
3. Fold in the sides of each wrap, then roll tightly to enclose the filling. Slice each wrap in half on a diagonal for easy serving. Serve immediately, or wrap tightly in parchment paper and refrigerate for up to 4 hours.

Nutritional Information (per serving)

- Calories: 290 kcal
- Total Fat: 15g
- Saturated Fat: 3.5g
- Carbohydrates: 28g
- Protein: 8g
- Fiber: 6g
- Sugar: 5g
- Salt: 400mg

Air-Fried Chickpea Crunch

Prep Time: 10 minutes   **Cook Time:** 15 minutes   **Servings:** 4

Ingredients

- **1 can (400g) chickpeas, drained and rinsed**
- **1 tablespoon olive oil**
- **1 teaspoon smoked paprika**
- **1 teaspoon garlic powder**
- **½ teaspoon ground cumin**
- **½ teaspoon salt**
- **¼ teaspoon black pepper**

Instructions

1. Pat the chickpeas dry using a clean kitchen towel or paper towel to remove excess moisture. This helps them crisp up during cooking. Transfer the dried chickpeas to a bowl and toss them with olive oil until well coated. Add the smoked paprika, garlic powder, cumin, salt, and black pepper to the bowl, and mix thoroughly so the chickpeas are evenly coated with the seasoning.

2. Preheat your air fryer to 180°C (350°F) for 2-3 minutes. Place the seasoned chickpeas in a single layer in the air fryer basket, ensuring they are not overcrowded. Cook the chickpeas for 15 minutes, shaking the basket every 5 minutes to ensure even cooking. Check for doneness; they should be golden brown and crunchy.

3. Allow the chickpeas to cool slightly before serving. They will become even crunchier as they cool. Serve as a snack, salad topping, or healthy alternative to croutons.

Nutritional Information (per serving)

- Calories: 120 kcal
- Total Fat: 5g
- Saturated Fat: 0.5g
- Carbohydrates: 14g
- Protein: 5g
- Fiber: 4g
- Sugar: 1g
- Salt: 250mg

Edamame Hummus with Crudités

Prep Time: 10 minutes   **Cook Time:** 5 minutes   **Servings:** 4

Ingredients

For the Hummus:
- **250g shelled edamame beans (frozen or fresh)**
- **2 tablespoons tahini**
- **2 tablespoons extra-virgin olive oil**
- **2 tablespoons fresh lemon juice**
- **1 clove garlic, minced**
- **1/2 teaspoon ground cumin**
- **1/4 teaspoon salt (or to taste)**
- **3-4 tablespoons water (adjust for consistency)**

For the Crudités:
- **1 medium carrot, cut into sticks**
- **1 celery stalk, cut into sticks**
- **1 red bell pepper, cut into strips**
- **1 cucumber, sliced into rounds**
- **8 radishes, halved**

Instructions

1. Cook the edamame beans by boiling them in salted water for 4-5 minutes until tender. Drain the beans and run them under cold water to cool. In a food processor, combine the edamame beans, tahini, olive oil, lemon juice, garlic, cumin, and salt. Blend the mixture until smooth, adding water one tablespoon at a time to achieve your desired consistency.
2. Adjust seasoning with additional salt or lemon juice, if necessary. Transfer the hummus to a serving bowl and drizzle with a bit of olive oil for presentation.
3. Arrange the prepared crudités on a platter or around the hummus for dipping and serve immediately.

Nutritional Information:

- Calories: 190 kcal
- Total Fat: 10g
- Saturated Fat: 1.5g
- Carbohydrates: 15g
- Protein: 7g
- Fiber: 5g
- Sugar: 4g
- Salt: 300mg

Sriracha Tuna Rice Bowls

Prep Time: 10 minutes   **Cook Time:** 15 minutes   **Servings:** 2

Ingredients

- **1 cup uncooked jasmine rice (or any preferred rice)**
- **1 can (160g) of tuna in water or brine, drained**
- **2 tablespoons mayonnaise (preferably light)**
- **1 tablespoon sriracha sauce (adjust to taste)**
- **1 teaspoon soy sauce**
- **1 teaspoon sesame oil**
- **1 avocado, sliced**
- **1/2 cucumber, thinly sliced**
- **1 small carrot, julienned**
- **1 tablespoon sesame seeds**
- **1 spring onion, thinly sliced**
- **Nori sheets or seaweed snacks, cut into strips (optional)**

Instructions

1. Cook the rice according to the package instructions. Once cooked, fluff with a fork and divide between two bowls. In a small bowl, mix the drained tuna with mayonnaise, sriracha sauce, and soy sauce until well combined.
2. Adjust the level of sriracha according to your spice preference. Drizzle sesame oil over the warm rice in each bowl for added flavour.
3. Arrange the tuna mixture on top of the rice. Layer slices of avocado, cucumber, and carrot around the tuna. Sprinkle sesame seeds and spring onion on top for garnish.
4. If desired, add strips of nori sheets or seaweed snacks for an extra burst of umami.

Nutritional Information (per serving)

- Calories: 430 kcal
- Total Fat: 19g
- Saturated Fat: 3g
- Carbohydrates: 42g
- Protein: 22g
- Fiber: 6g
- Sugar: 3g
- Salt: 700mg

Greek Yoghurt Berry Bark

Prep Time: 10 minutes   **Cook Time:** 0 minutes   **Servings:** 6

Ingredients

- **500g Greek yoghurt (plain or vanilla)**
- **2 tablespoons honey or maple syrup (optional, for sweetness)**
- **1 cup mixed fresh berries (e.g., strawberries, blueberries, raspberries)**
- **2 tablespoons chopped nuts (e.g., almonds or pistachios)**
- **1 tablespoon desiccated coconut (optional)**
- **1 teaspoon chia seeds (optional)**

Instructions

1. Line a baking tray or a flat dish with parchment paper to prevent sticking. In a mixing bowl, combine the Greek yoghurt with honey or maple syrup if you prefer a slightly sweeter bark.
2. Spread the yoghurt mixture evenly onto the prepared tray, ensuring it's about 1cm thick. Scatter the mixed berries evenly over the yoghurt base, pressing them lightly so they adhere.
3. Sprinkle the chopped nuts, desiccated coconut, and chia seeds over the top for added texture and flavour. Place the tray in the freezer and let it freeze for at least 2 hours or until the yoghurt is firm.
4. Once frozen, break the bark into pieces and serve immediately or store in an airtight container in the freezer for up to a week.

Nutritional Information (per serving)

- Calories: 110 kcal
- Total Fat: 4g
- Saturated Fat: 1g
- Carbohydrates: 9g
- Protein: 8g
- Fiber: 2g
- Sugar: 6g
- Salt: 40mg

Vegan Lentil & Sweet Potato Stew

Prep Time: 15 minutes   **Cook Time:** 40 minutes   **Servings:** 4

Ingredients

- **2 tablespoons olive oil**
- **1 large onion, finely chopped**
- **2 garlic cloves, minced**
- **2 medium sweet potatoes, peeled and diced**
- **2 medium carrots, diced**
- **1 cup dried red lentils, rinsed**
- **1 tin (400g) chopped tomatoes**
- **1 tin (400ml) coconut milk**
- **750ml vegetable stock**
- **1 teaspoon ground cumin**
- **1 teaspoon smoked paprika**
- **1/2 teaspoon ground cinnamon**
- **1/2 teaspoon ground turmeric**
- **Salt and black pepper, to taste**
- **Juice of 1 lemon**
- **Fresh coriander, chopped, for garnish**

Instructions

1. Heat the olive oil in a large pot over medium heat. Add the onion and garlic, cooking until softened and fragrant, about 3-5 minutes. Stir in the diced sweet potatoes and carrots, and cook for another 5 minutes, stirring occasionally. Add the spices, including cumin, smoked paprika, cinnamon, and turmeric, and cook for 1-2 minutes to release their flavours.
2. Stir in the rinsed lentils, chopped tomatoes, coconut milk, and vegetable stock. Bring the mixture to a boil, then reduce the heat to low, cover the pot, and simmer for 25-30 minutes, stirring occasionally. The lentils should be tender, and the sweet potatoes should be soft.
3. Season the stew with salt, black pepper, and lemon juice, adjusting to taste. Serve hot, garnished with fresh coriander.

Nutritional Information (per serving)

- Calories: 380 kcal
- Total Fat: 14g
- Saturated Fat: 9g
- Carbohydrates: 50g
- Protein: 12g
- Fiber: 12g
- Sugar: 11g
- Salt: 600mg

TikTok Watermelon Pizza

Prep Time: 10 minutes   **Cook Time:** None   **Servings:** 4

Ingredients

- **1 large round watermelon slice (about 1 inch thick)**
- **200g Greek yoghurt (plain or flavoured)**
- **1 tbsp honey (optional)**
- **1 cup mixed fresh fruit (e.g., berries,**

kiwi, mango, or grapes), diced
- 2 tbsp granola
- Fresh mint leaves, for garnish

Instructions

1. Place the watermelon slice on a cutting board and pat it dry with a kitchen towel to remove excess moisture. Spread an even layer of Greek yoghurt over the top of the watermelon slice, covering the surface completely.
2. If you like a sweeter taste, mix the Greek yoghurt with honey before spreading. Arrange the diced fruit on top of the yoghurt, creating a colourful and appealing pattern. Sprinkle granola over the fruit for added crunch and texture.
3. Garnish with fresh mint leaves for a burst of freshness. Slice the watermelon into wedges, as you would a pizza, and serve immediately.

Nutritional Information (per serving)

- Calories: 120 kcal
- Total Fat: 3g
- Saturated Fat: 1g
- Carbohydrates: 22g
- Protein: 5g
- Fiber: 2g
- Sugar: 17g
- Salt: 40mg

Protein Peanut Butter Cookies

Prep Time: 10 minutes   **Cook Time:** 12 minutes   **Servings:** 12 cookies

Ingredients

- 1 cup of rolled oats
- 1/2 cup of peanut butter
- 1/4 cup of honey (or maple syrup)
- 1 scoop of vanilla protein powder
- 1 large egg
- 1 teaspoon of vanilla extract
- 1/4 teaspoon of baking soda
- Optional: chocolate chips for extra sweetness

Instructions

1. Preheat the oven to 180°C (350°F) and line a baking sheet with parchment paper.
2. In a food processor or blender, pulse the oats until they form a coarse flour texture.
3. In a large mixing bowl, combine the oat flour, peanut butter, honey, egg, and vanilla extract. Mix until well combined.
4. Stir in the protein powder, baking soda, and any optional chocolate chips until evenly distributed.
5. Roll the mixture into balls, about 1.5 tablespoons in size, and place them onto the baking sheet.
6. Flatten each ball slightly with a fork to create a criss-cross pattern on top of the cookies.
7. Bake in the preheated oven for 12 minutes, or until the edges start to turn golden brown.

8. Allow the cookies to cool on the baking sheet for 5 minutes before transferring them to a wire rack to cool completely.

Nutritional Information (per cookie)
- Calories: 150 kcal
- Total Fat: 8g
- Saturated Fat: 3g
- Carbohydrates: 15g
- Protein: 8g
- Fiber: 2g
- Sugar: 8g
- Salt: 50mg

Matcha Energy Bites

Prep Time: 10 minutes   **Cook Time:** 0 minutes   **Servings:** 12-14 bites

Ingredients
- **1 cup rolled oats**
- **2 tablespoons matcha powder**
- **1/4 cup almond butter (or any nut butter of choice)**
- **2 tablespoons honey or maple syrup**
- **1/4 cup unsweetened desiccated coconut**
- **1/4 cup chia seeds**
- **1/4 cup dark chocolate chips (optional)**
- **1/2 teaspoon vanilla extract**
- **Pinch of salt**

Instructions
1. In a medium bowl, combine the rolled oats, matcha powder, and desiccated coconut. Stir in the almond butter, honey (or maple syrup), and vanilla extract.
2. Add the chia seeds, chocolate chips (if using), and a pinch of salt. Mix everything together until the ingredients are fully combined and a sticky dough forms. If the mixture feels too dry, add a little more honey or almond butter to reach a dough-like consistency.
3. Roll the mixture into small bite-sized balls, about 1 inch in diameter. Place the bites on a tray lined with parchment paper. Once all the bites are rolled, refrigerate for at least 30 minutes to firm up.
4. Serve chilled or at room temperature. Store the energy bites in an airtight container in the fridge for up to one week.

Nutritional Information (per serving, 1 bite)
- Calories: 90 kcal
- Total Fat: 6g
- Saturated Fat: 1g
- Carbohydrates: 8g
- Protein: 2g
- Fiber: 2g
- Sugar: 3g
- Salt: 0.1g

Avocado Salsa Bowls

Prep Time: 15 minutes   **Cook Time:** 0 minutes   **Servings:** 2

Ingredients

- 2 ripe avocados, peeled, pitted, and diced
- 1 medium tomato, diced
- 1/2 red onion, finely diced
- 1/2 cucumber, diced
- 1/4 cup fresh coriander (cilantro), chopped
- 1 lime, juiced
- 1 tbsp olive oil
- Salt and pepper, to taste
- 1 small red chili, finely chopped (optional)
- 2 small bowls or avocado halves (to serve)
- 1/2 cup tortilla chips, crumbled (optional)

Instructions

1. Start by preparing the vegetables. Dice the avocados, tomato, red onion, and cucumber.
2. Place them into a large mixing bowl. Add the chopped coriander, lime juice, olive oil, and season with salt and pepper to taste. If desired, add the finely chopped chili for a bit of heat. Gently toss the ingredients together, being careful not to mash the avocado too much.
3. Once the salsa is well combined, spoon it into two small bowls or the empty avocado halves, if using.
4. For an extra crunch, sprinkle the crumbled tortilla chips over the top and serve immediately.

Nutritional Information (per serving)

- Calories: 350 kcal
- Total Fat: 28g
- Saturated Fat: 4g
- Carbohydrates: 22g
- Protein: 5g
- Fiber: 12g
- Sugar: 4g
- Salt: 200mg

Air-Fried Veggie Nuggets

Prep Time: 15 minutes   **Cook Time:** 15 minutes   **Servings:** 4

Ingredients

- 1 cup of cooked sweet potato, mashed
- 1/2 cup of grated carrot
- 1/2 cup of cooked broccoli, finely chopped
- 1/2 cup of breadcrumbs (use gluten-free if needed)
- 1/4 cup of grated cheddar cheese (optional)
- 1 egg
- 1 teaspoon of garlic powder

- 1 teaspoon of dried oregano
- Salt and pepper, to taste
- Olive oil spray

Instructions

1. To begin, preheat the air fryer to 180°C. In a large mixing bowl, combine the mashed sweet potato, grated carrot, chopped broccoli, breadcrumbs, cheese (if using), egg, garlic powder, oregano, salt, and pepper. Mix everything together until well combined.
2. Next, shape the mixture into small nugget-sized portions, about 1 to 2 tablespoons per nugget. Arrange the nuggets in a single layer in the air fryer basket, ensuring they don't touch each other.
3. Lightly spray the nuggets with olive oil to help them crisp up. Air fry the veggie nuggets at 180°C for about 12-15 minutes, or until golden brown and crispy on the outside, flipping them halfway through for even cooking.
4. Once done, remove the nuggets from the air fryer and serve immediately with your favourite dipping sauce.

Nutritional Information (per serving)

- Calories: 190 kcal
- Total Fat: 8g
- Saturated Fat: 2g
- Carbohydrates: 26g
- Protein: 5g
- Fiber: 6g
- Sugar: 6g
- Salt: 250mg

Zoodle Pad Thai

Prep Time: 15 minutes   **Cook Time:** 10 minutes   **Servings:** 2

Ingredients

- **2 medium zucchinis (for zoodles)**
- **200g cooked chicken breast (or tofu for a vegetarian option)**
- **2 eggs, lightly beaten**
- **1/2 red bell pepper, thinly sliced**
- **1 small carrot, julienned**
- **2 spring onions, chopped**
- **2 cloves garlic, minced**
- **2 tbsp peanut butter**
- **1 tbsp soy sauce**
- **1 tbsp fish sauce (optional, or extra soy sauce for a vegetarian option)**
- **1 tbsp lime juice**
- **1 tsp brown sugar**
- **1 tbsp sesame oil**
- **1 tbsp olive oil (for cooking)**
- **1/4 cup roasted peanuts, chopped (for garnish)**
- **1 lime, cut into wedges (for serving)**
- **Fresh coriander (optional, for garnish)**

Instructions

1. To make the zoodles, use a spiralizer to turn the zucchinis into noodles. Alternatively, use a julienne peeler. Set the zoodles aside.
2. In a small bowl, mix together the peanut butter, soy sauce, fish sauce, lime juice, and brown sugar to make the Pad Thai sauce. Stir until smooth and set aside.
3. Heat the olive oil in a large frying pan or wok over medium heat. Add the garlic and cook for 1 minute until fragrant. Add the chicken (or tofu) and cook for 2-3 minutes until heated through. Push the chicken to one side of the pan.
4. In the same pan, pour in the beaten eggs and scramble them until fully cooked. Add the red bell pepper, carrot, and spring onions to the pan, cooking for an additional 2-3 minutes until slightly softened.
5. Add the zoodles to the pan along with the Pad Thai sauce. Toss everything together to combine and cook for 2-3 minutes, until the zoodles are just tender but still have a bite.
6. Serve the Zoodle Pad Thai in bowls, garnished with chopped peanuts, lime wedges, and fresh coriander if desired.

Nutritional Information (per serving)

- Calories: 350 kcal
- Total Fat: 18g
- Saturated Fat: 3g
- Carbohydrates: 28g
- Protein: 20g
- Fiber: 5g
- Sugar: 8g
- Salt: 650mg

TikTok Shakshuka Cups

Prep Time: 10 minutes   **Cook Time:** 20 minutes   **Servings:** 4

Ingredients

- 4 large eggs
- 1 can (400g) chopped tomatoes
- 1 medium onion, diced
- 1 bell pepper, diced
- 1 clove garlic, minced
- 1 tsp ground cumin
- 1 tsp paprika
- 1 tsp chili flakes (optional)
- 1 tbsp olive oil
- 4 whole wheat or white flour tortillas
- Salt and pepper, to taste
- Fresh parsley, chopped (for garnish)
- Crumbled feta cheese (optional, for garnish)

Instructions

1. Preheat Oven and Prepare Tortilla Cups: Preheat your oven to 180°C (160°C fan) or 350°F. Lightly grease a muffin tin. Cut the tortillas into 4 rounds, large enough to line the muffin cups. Press each round into the tin to form tortilla cups and bake for 8-10 minutes until crispy and golden. Set aside.

2. Cook Vegetables: In a large pan, heat olive oil over medium heat. Add the diced onion and bell pepper, cooking for 5-7 minutes until softened. Add the minced garlic, cumin, paprika, and chili flakes (if using), cooking for another 1 minute until fragrant.
3. Add Tomatoes and Simmer: Pour in the chopped tomatoes, season with salt and pepper, and bring to a simmer. Let the mixture cook for about 10 minutes, allowing the sauce to thicken and the flavours to meld together.
4. Assemble Shakshuka Cups: Once the tomato mixture is ready, carefully spoon it into the baked tortilla cups, filling them almost to the top. Make a small well in the centre of each cup.
5. Add Eggs: Crack an egg into each well of the tortilla cups. Return the pan to the oven and bake for 10-12 minutes, or until the egg whites are set but the yolks are still runny.
6. Garnish and Serve: Remove the shakshuka cups from the oven. Garnish with fresh parsley and crumbled feta cheese if desired. Serve immediately with your favourite side or toasted bread.

Nutritional Information (per serving)

- Calories: 220 kcal
- Total Fat: 13g
- Saturated Fat: 3g
- Carbohydrates: 18g
- Protein: 9g
- Fiber: 3g
- Sugar: 6g
- Salt: 250mg

Low-Cal Chocolate Mug Cake

Prep Time: 5 minutes   **Cook Time:** 1-2 minutes   **Servings:** 1

Ingredients

- 2 tbsp cocoa powder
- 3 tbsp self-raising flour
- 1 tbsp sweetener (such as stevia or erythritol)
- 1/4 tsp baking powder
- Pinch of salt
- 3 tbsp unsweetened almond milk (or milk of choice)
- 1 tbsp Greek yogurt
- 1 tsp vanilla extract
- 1/2 tbsp vegetable oil or melted coconut oil

Instructions

1. In a microwave-safe mug, combine cocoa powder, self-raising flour, sweetener, baking powder, and a pinch of salt. Stir the dry ingredients together until fully mixed.
2. Add almond milk, Greek yogurt, vanilla extract, and vegetable oil to the dry ingredients and stir until smooth. Make sure there are no lumps and the batter is thick but pourable.

3. Microwave the mug on high for 1 minute, then check the cake's doneness. If it's not fully cooked, microwave in 10-15 second intervals until the cake has risen and a toothpick comes out clean.
4. Let it cool for a minute before serving. Enjoy straight from the mug, topped with a dusting of cocoa or a dollop of low-fat whipped cream if desired.

Nutritional Information (per serving)

- Calories: 150 kcal
- Total Fat: 7g
- Saturated Fat: 2g
- Carbohydrates: 19g
- Protein: 6g
- Fiber: 3g
- Sugar: 3g
- Salt: 200mg

DRINKS THAT SLAY

TikTok Pink Drink Smoothie

Prep Time: 5 minutes   **Cook Time:** 0 minutes   **Servings:** 2

Ingredients
- 1 cup frozen strawberries
- 1/2 cup coconut milk (or coconut water for a lighter option)
- 1/2 cup ice cubes
- 1/2 cup almond milk (or any milk of your choice)
- 1 tbsp honey or maple syrup (optional)
- 1/2 tsp vanilla extract
- 1/4 cup Greek yoghurt (for creaminess)
- 1–2 tbsp freeze-dried strawberries (optional, for extra pink colour and flavour)

Instructions
1. Combine the frozen strawberries, coconut milk, almond milk, ice cubes, honey or maple syrup, vanilla extract, and Greek yoghurt into a blender. Blend until smooth and creamy.
2. For a thicker consistency, add more frozen strawberries or ice. If you prefer a more vibrant pink colour, add freeze-dried strawberries and blend again.
3. Pour into glasses and serve immediately. Garnish with additional freeze-dried strawberries or a few fresh strawberry slices for an extra touch of pink.

Nutritional Information (per serving)
- Calories: 180 kcal
- Total Fat: 9g
- Saturated Fat: 5g
- Carbohydrates: 24g
- Sugar: 18g
- Protein: 5g
- Fiber: 4g
- Salt: 0.2g

Fancy Whipped Lemonade

Prep Time: 10 minutes   **Cook Time:** 0 minutes   **Servings:** 2

Ingredients
- 1 cup (240ml) cold water
- 1/2 cup (120ml) fresh lemon juice (about 2 lemons)
- 2 tablespoons powdered sugar (or to taste)

- 1/2 cup (120ml) double cream
- 1 tablespoon honey or maple syrup
- Ice cubes
- Lemon slices, for garnish
- Fresh mint leaves, for garnish

Instructions

1. To start, in a bowl, whisk together the cold water, fresh lemon juice, and powdered sugar until the sugar dissolves completely. In a separate bowl, whip the double cream and honey (or maple syrup) together using a hand mixer or whisk until soft peaks form.

2. Once the cream is whipped, gently stir in the whipped cream mixture into the lemon water mixture, leaving some cream peaks visible for a fluffy texture. Add ice cubes to two glasses, then pour the whipped lemonade mixture over the ice.

3. Garnish each glass with a slice of lemon and a sprig of fresh mint. Serve immediately and enjoy this refreshing treat!

Nutritional Information (per serving)

- Calories: 180 kcal
- Total Fat: 16g
- Saturated Fat: 10g
- Carbohydrates: 10g
- Sugar: 9g
- Protein: 1g
- Fiber: 0g
- Salt: 30mg

Colour-Changing Butterfly Pea Tea

Prep Time: 5 minutes   **Cook Time:** 0 minutes   **Servings:** 2

Ingredients

- 2 teaspoons dried butterfly pea flowers
- 500ml boiling water
- 1 tablespoon honey or sweetener of choice (optional)
- 1 tablespoon fresh lemon juice
- Ice cubes (optional)

Instructions

1. Start by placing the dried butterfly pea flowers into a heatproof container or a teapot. Pour 500ml of boiling water over the flowers and let them steep for about 5 minutes. As the tea steeps, it will turn a deep blue color. Once the tea has cooled slightly, strain out the flowers. If you prefer your tea sweetened, add honey or another sweetener to taste, stirring until fully dissolved. For a chilled version, pour the tea into a glass over ice cubes. Add a tablespoon of fresh lemon juice just before serving. Watch as the tea changes color from blue to a beautiful purple or pink hue, depending on the acidity of the lemon juice.

Nutritional Information (per serving)

- Calories: 20 kcal
- Total Fat: 0g
- Saturated Fat: 0g
- Carbohydrates: 5g
- Protein: 0g
- Fiber: 0g
- Sugar: 5g
- Salt: 0mg

Iced Matcha Latte Perfection

Prep Time: 5 minutes   **Cook Time:** 0 minutes   **Servings:** 1

Ingredients
- 1 tsp matcha powder
- 2 oz hot water
- 1 cup cold milk (dairy or plant-based)
- 1-2 tsp honey or sweetener (optional)
- Ice cubes

Instructions
1. Start by sifting 1 tsp of matcha powder into a small bowl to avoid any lumps. Pour 2 oz of hot water over the matcha powder and whisk vigorously for about 30 seconds, using a matcha whisk or a small regular whisk, until the matcha is fully dissolved and frothy. Add honey or your preferred sweetener and mix well.
2. Fill a glass with ice cubes, then pour the cold milk into the glass, leaving a little space at the top. Gently pour the whisked matcha mixture over the milk. Stir to combine, and your iced matcha latte is ready to serve.
3. For an extra touch, you can add a few more ice cubes or top with a bit of frothy milk for an added texture.

Nutritional Information (per serving)
- Calories: 80 kcal (with plant-based milk)
- Total Fat: 2g
- Saturated Fat: 0g
- Carbohydrates: 12g
- Protein: 4g
- Fiber: 0g
- Sugar: 6g (if sweetener is added)
- Salt: 0g

Fizzy Watermelon Mojito

Prep Time: 10 minutes   **Cook Time:** 0 minutes   **Servings:** 2

Ingredients
- **2 cups watermelon, cubed**
- **1/4 cup fresh mint leaves**
- **1 lime, cut into wedges**
- **2 teaspoons honey or sugar (optional)**
- **200ml soda water or sparkling water**
- **Ice cubes**
- **2 shots white rum (optional)**

- Mint sprigs and lime slices, for garnish

Instructions

1. Start by placing the watermelon cubes in a blender and blending until smooth. Strain the watermelon juice through a fine mesh sieve into a jug, discarding any pulp.
2. Add the fresh mint leaves to the jug, along with the lime wedges and honey (or sugar), and use a muddler or back of a spoon to gently crush the mint and lime to release their juices.
3. Fill two glasses with ice cubes, then pour the watermelon-mint mixture evenly into the glasses. Top each glass with soda water or sparkling water, and stir gently to combine. If using rum, pour a shot into each glass before stirring.
4. Garnish with extra mint sprigs and lime slices. Serve immediately and enjoy!

Nutritional Information (per serving)

- Calories: 95 kcal
- Total Fat: 0g
- Saturated Fat: 0g
- Carbohydrates: 25g
- Protein: 1g
- Fiber: 2g
- Sugar: 21g
- Salt: 5mg

TikTok Boba Tea Creations

Prep Time: 10 minutes   **Cook Time:** 10 minutes   **Servings:** 2

Ingredients

- 100g black tapioca pearls
- 500ml brewed black tea (or green tea if preferred)
- 200ml milk (or dairy-free milk like oat, almond, or coconut)
- 2 tablespoons sugar syrup (or honey, to taste)
- Ice cubes
- Optional: flavoured syrups or fruit purée for variety (e.g., strawberry, mango, or matcha)

Instructions

1. To start, bring a pot of water to a boil. Add the tapioca pearls and cook according to the instructions on the packaging, usually for about 5-10 minutes until they become soft and chewy. Once done, drain the pearls and rinse them under cold water to remove excess starch. If you want to add a sweet touch, drizzle some sugar syrup or honey over the cooked pearls and mix gently.
2. While the pearls are cooking, brew the tea. For a stronger flavour, steep the tea for 3-5 minutes, then remove the tea bags or leaves. Let the tea cool for a few minutes before adding the milk. If you prefer a sweeter taste, mix in a tablespoon or two of sugar syrup or honey to your brewed tea, adjusting to your sweetness preference.

3. In a separate glass, add a handful of ice cubes. Spoon the sweetened tapioca pearls into the glass and pour the milk-tea mixture over the ice and pearls. Stir the drink thoroughly to combine the flavours.
4. For added creativity, try mixing in a fruit purée or flavoured syrup like strawberry, mango, or matcha for a fruity or flavoured twist to your boba tea. Top with extra ice or serve with a straw, and enjoy your TikTok-inspired boba tea creation.

Nutritional Information (per serving)
- Calories: 180 kcal (without sweeteners or fruit purée)
- Total Fat: 3g
- Saturated Fat: 1g
- Carbohydrates: 35g
- Protein: 3g
- Fiber: 2g
- Sugar: 18g
- Salt: 10mg

Creamy Nutella Hot Chocolate

Prep Time: 5 minutes   **Cook Time:** 5 minutes   **Servings:** 2

Ingredients
- **2 cups whole milk**
- **3 tbsp Nutella**
- **50g milk chocolate, chopped**
- **1/2 tsp vanilla extract**
- **Whipped cream, for topping (optional)**
- **Grated chocolate or cocoa powder, for garnish (optional)**

Instructions
1. To start, heat the milk in a medium-sized saucepan over medium heat. Once the milk begins to warm up, whisk in the Nutella until fully melted and smooth. Add the chopped milk chocolate and stir until completely dissolved, creating a creamy, rich texture.
2. Continue heating the mixture, stirring constantly, until it reaches a steaming temperature but before it starts boiling. Remove from heat and add the vanilla extract, stirring to combine.
3. Pour the hot chocolate into two mugs and top with whipped cream, if desired. Garnish with grated chocolate or a sprinkle of cocoa powder for extra indulgence. Serve hot and enjoy!

Nutritional Information (per serving)
- Calories: 380 kcal
- Total Fat: 19g
- Saturated Fat: 10g
- Carbohydrates: 45g
- Sugars: 40g
- Protein: 7g
- Fiber: 2g
- Salt: 0.1g

Strawberry Prosecco Spritzers

Prep Time: 10 minutes   **Cook Time:** 0 minutes   **Servings:** 4

Ingredients

- 200g fresh strawberries, hulled and sliced
- 2 tbsp honey or simple syrup (optional)
- 1 tbsp lemon juice
- 500ml Prosecco
- 200ml soda water or sparkling water
- Fresh mint leaves, for garnish
- Ice cubes

Instructions

1. In a blender or food processor, blend the fresh strawberries until smooth. If you prefer a sweeter drink, add honey or simple syrup to taste and blend again. Pour the strawberry puree into a large jug or bowl, and stir in the lemon juice.
2. Fill four glasses with ice cubes, then pour the strawberry mixture evenly into each glass. Top each glass with Prosecco, filling it about three-quarters full, and add a splash of soda water or sparkling water for extra fizz. Stir gently to combine, then garnish with a sprig of fresh mint. Serve immediately.

Nutritional Information (per serving)

- Calories: 130 kcal
- Total Fat: 0g
- Saturated Fat: 0g
- Carbohydrates: 10g
- Sugar: 9g
- Protein: 0g
- Fiber: 1g
- Salt: 5mg

Layered Mango Sunrise Slushie

Prep Time: 10 minutes   **Cook Time:** None   **Servings:** 2

Ingredients

- 1 ripe mango, peeled and chopped
- 200ml fresh orange juice
- 100g frozen raspberries
- 1 tablespoon honey or maple syrup (optional)
- Ice cubes (about 1.5 cups)
- 50ml water

Instructions

1. To make the mango layer, blend the ripe mango with orange juice and ice cubes until smooth and thick. If needed, add a small amount of water to help the blender process. Taste and adjust sweetness with honey or maple syrup, if desired. Pour the mango mixture into glasses, filling them about halfway.

2. For the raspberry layer, blend the frozen raspberries with ice cubes and a splash of water until smooth. Carefully spoon the raspberry slushie over the back of a spoon, layering it gently on top of the mango layer to create a sunrise effect.
3. Serve immediately with a straw or spoon and enjoy the refreshing, layered slushie.

Nutritional Information (per serving)

- Calories: 140 kcal
- Total Fat: 1g
- Saturated Fat: 0g
- Carbohydrates: 35g
- Protein: 2g
- Fiber: 5g
- Sugar: 25g
- Salt: 0g

Tiramisu Milkshake

Prep Time: 5 minutes   **Cook Time:** 0 minutes   **Servings:** 2

Ingredients

- **3 scoops vanilla ice cream**
- **1/2 cup strong brewed coffee, cooled**
- **1/2 cup milk**
- **2 tbsp mascarpone cheese**
- **1 tbsp sugar (optional)**
- **1/2 tsp vanilla extract**
- **2 tbsp cocoa powder (for dusting)**
- **Crushed biscuits (optional, for garnish)**

Instructions

1. In a blender, combine the vanilla ice cream, cooled brewed coffee, milk, mascarpone cheese, sugar (if using), and vanilla extract. Blend until smooth and creamy. Taste and adjust sweetness if needed by adding more sugar.
2. Pour the milkshake into two glasses and sprinkle a light dusting of cocoa powder on top. Optionally, you can garnish with crushed biscuits for an extra touch of texture and flavour.
3. Serve immediately and enjoy this indulgent twist on the classic tiramisu!

Nutritional Information (per serving)

- Calories: 450 kcal
- Total Fat: 22g
- Saturated Fat: 14g
- Carbohydrates: 54g
- Protein: 7g
- Fiber: 2g
- Sugar: 42g
- Salt: 80mg

Blueberry Lavender Soda

Prep Time: 10 minutes   **Cook Time:** 5 minutes   **Servings:** 4

Ingredients

- **200g fresh blueberries**
- **2 tsp dried lavender flowers**
- **2 tbsp honey (or to taste)**
- **1 litre sparkling water**
- **1 tbsp lemon juice**
- **Ice cubes**
- **Fresh lavender sprigs (for garnish, optional)**
- **Lemon slices (for garnish, optional)**

Instructions

1. In a small saucepan, combine the blueberries, dried lavender, and honey with 100ml of water. Heat over medium heat, stirring occasionally, until the blueberries begin to burst and release their juices, about 3-4 minutes. Remove from the heat and let the mixture steep for another 5 minutes to infuse the flavours. Strain the mixture through a fine mesh sieve into a jug, pressing the blueberries to extract all the juice.

2. Add the lemon juice to the blueberry-lavender syrup and stir well. Fill four glasses with ice cubes, then pour the blueberry-lavender syrup evenly into each glass, about 2-3 tablespoons per glass.

3. Top each glass with sparkling water and stir gently to combine. Garnish with fresh lavender sprigs and lemon slices if desired. Serve immediately and enjoy the refreshing flavours.

Nutritional Information (per serving)

- Calories: 50 kcal
- Total Fat: 0g
- Saturated Fat: 0g
- Carbohydrates: 12g
- Sugar: 11g
- Protein: 0g
- Fiber: 1g
- Salt: 0mg

Raspberry Mint Lemonade

Prep Time: 10 minutes   **Cook Time:** 0 minutes   **Servings:** 4

Ingredients

- **200g fresh raspberries**
- **1 handful of fresh mint leaves**
- **4 large lemons (juiced)**
- **500ml cold water**
- **2 tbsp honey or sugar (to taste)**
- **Ice cubes, as needed**
- **Mint sprigs for garnish**
- **Lemon slices for garnish**

Instructions

1. To prepare the raspberry mint lemonade, begin by placing the raspberries and mint leaves in a blender. Add a small amount of cold water and blend until smooth.

2. Once blended, pour the mixture through a fine sieve to remove the seeds, collecting the juice in a jug. Next, squeeze the juice from the lemons into the jug, adding the remaining cold water.
3. Stir in the honey or sugar, adjusting to your desired sweetness. Add ice cubes to the jug and stir to chill the lemonade. Finally, pour the lemonade into glasses, garnishing with fresh mint sprigs and lemon slices.

Nutritional Information (per serving)

- Calories: 70 kcal
- Total Fat: 0g
- Saturated Fat: 0g
- Carbohydrates: 18g
- Sugars: 16g
- Protein: 1g
- Fiber: 2g
- Salt: 1mg

Spiced Chai Iced Latte

Prep Time: 5 minutes   **Cook Time:** 5 minutes   **Servings:** 1

Ingredients

- **1 chai tea bag**
- **250ml boiling water**
- **200ml milk (or plant-based milk of choice)**
- **1-2 teaspoons honey or sweetener (optional)**
- **Ice cubes**
- **Ground cinnamon (for garnish)**
- **Ground ginger (optional, for extra spice)**

Instructions

1. Brew the chai tea by placing the tea bag in a cup and pouring over the boiling water. Let it steep for about 5 minutes, then remove the tea bag.
2. Allow the tea to cool for a few minutes, or place it in the fridge to speed up the process. In a separate glass, fill with ice cubes.
3. Once the tea has cooled, pour it over the ice-filled glass. In a small saucepan, heat the milk over medium heat until warm (don't boil). Once heated, froth the milk using a milk frother or whisk it vigorously until frothy. Pour the frothy milk into the glass with the chai tea.
4. Stir in honey or sweetener if desired, and sprinkle a pinch of cinnamon on top for garnish. Optionally, add a pinch of ground ginger for an extra spiced kick.

Nutritional Information (per serving)

- Calories: 150 kcal
- Total Fat: 6g
- Saturated Fat: 3g
- Carbohydrates: 18g
- Protein: 4g
- Fiber: 0g
- Sugar: 12g
- Salt: 50mg

TikTok Coffee Jelly Frappe

Prep Time: 15 minutes   **Cook Time:** 5 minutes   **Servings:** 2

Ingredients

- 1 cup strong brewed coffee (cooled)
- 1 tablespoon instant coffee granules
- 1 tablespoon sugar (optional, or adjust to taste)
- 1 teaspoon agar-agar powder
- 1 cup ice cubes
- 1/2 cup milk (or plant-based milk)
- 1 tablespoon sugar syrup or honey (optional)
- Whipped cream, for topping (optional)

Instructions

1. To make the coffee jelly, dissolve the agar-agar powder in the brewed coffee and sugar in a saucepan over low heat. Stir until the agar-agar is completely dissolved, then bring the mixture to a boil for 1-2 minutes. Pour the mixture into a shallow dish or silicone mould and allow it to set at room temperature for about 30 minutes or until firm.
2. Once the jelly has set, cut it into small cubes. In a blender, combine the ice cubes, milk, sugar syrup (or honey), and a few coffee jelly cubes. Blend until smooth and frothy.
3. Pour the frappe mixture into glasses and add more coffee jelly cubes for texture. Top with whipped cream for an extra indulgent touch, and garnish with a sprinkle of instant coffee or cocoa powder if desired.

Nutritional Information (per serving)

- Calories: 180 kcal
- Total Fat: 8g
- Saturated Fat: 4g
- Carbohydrates: 24g
- Protein: 3g
- Fiber: 1g
- Sugar: 20g
- Salt: 50mg

Unicorn Cotton Candy Float

Prep Time: 5 minutes   **Cook Time:** 0 minutes   **Servings:** 2

Ingredients

- 2 cups vanilla ice cream
- 1 cup pink lemonade
- 1/2 cup sparkling water
- 1/2 cup cotton candy (blue or pink)

- **2 maraschino cherries (optional)**
- **Whipped cream, for garnish**
- **Sprinkles (optional)**

Instructions

1. Start by placing one scoop of vanilla ice cream into each glass. Pour half a cup of pink lemonade into each glass, followed by sparkling water, filling up the glass. Stir gently to mix the liquids and create a fizzy effect.
2. Top each float with a generous swirl of whipped cream. Add cotton candy on top of the whipped cream, letting it melt slightly into the drink for a whimsical effect.
3. Garnish with sprinkles and a maraschino cherry if desired.

Nutritional Information (per serving)

- Calories: 320 kcal
- Total Fat: 15g
- Saturated Fat: 9g
- Carbohydrates: 41g
- Sugar: 39g
- Protein: 3g
- Fiber: 0g
- Salt: 10mg

PARTY FOOD & SHARING PLATES

Loaded Nacho Grazing Board

Prep Time: 15 minutes   **Cook Time:** 10 minutes   **Servings:** 6

Ingredients

- **200g tortilla chips**
- **150g grated cheddar cheese**
- **100g grated mozzarella cheese**
- **100g cooked chicken breast, shredded (optional)**
- **1 small red onion, finely chopped**
- **1 small red pepper, diced**
- **1 small green pepper, diced**
- **1 jalapeño, thinly sliced (optional)**
- **1 avocado, diced**
- **100g sour cream**
- **50g salsa**
- **Fresh coriander, for garnish**
- **1 lime, cut into wedges**
- **Salt and pepper, to taste**

Instructions

1. Preheat the oven to 180°C (160°C fan) or 350°F. On a large baking tray, arrange the tortilla chips in an even layer. Sprinkle the grated cheddar and mozzarella cheese generously over the chips. Add the shredded chicken, if using, and top with the diced red onion, red pepper, green pepper, and jalapeño slices.
2. Place the tray in the oven and bake for 8-10 minutes or until the cheese has melted and is bubbling. While the nachos are baking, prepare the toppings: dice the avocado, chop the coriander, and cut the lime into wedges.
3. Once the nachos are out of the oven, top them with the diced avocado, sour cream, salsa, and a sprinkle of fresh coriander. Serve with lime wedges on the side for extra zest. Season with salt and pepper to taste.

Nutritional Information (per serving)

- Calories: 450 kcal
- Total Fat: 25g
- Saturated Fat: 8g
- Carbohydrates: 40g
- Protein: 15g
- Fiber: 5g
- Sugar: 4g
- Salt: 600mg

Garlic Butter Bloom Bread

Prep Time: 15 minutes   **Cook Time:** 25 minutes   **Servings:** 6-8

Ingredients

- 1 large round loaf of sourdough bread
- 100g unsalted butter, melted
- 4 cloves garlic, minced
- 2 tbsp fresh parsley, chopped
- 1 tsp dried oregano
- 1 tsp dried thyme
- 100g grated mozzarella cheese
- Salt and pepper, to taste

Instructions

1. Preheat your oven to 180°C (350°F). Place the loaf of bread on a baking sheet. Using a sharp knife, make cuts across the bread both horizontally and vertically, creating a crisscross pattern without cutting all the way through the bottom.
2. In a small bowl, combine the melted butter, minced garlic, parsley, oregano, thyme, salt, and pepper. Stir well to combine.
3. Carefully pour or brush the garlic butter mixture into the cuts of the bread, making sure to get the butter into every nook and cranny. Then, stuff the grated mozzarella cheese between the slices of bread, ensuring an even distribution.
4. Cover the loaf loosely with aluminium foil and bake for 20 minutes. After 20 minutes, remove the foil and continue baking for an additional 5-10 minutes until the cheese is melted and the bread is golden and crispy.
5. Remove from the oven and allow to cool slightly before serving. Tear off pieces of the garlic butter bread and enjoy.

Nutritional Information (per serving)

- Calories: 290 kcal
- Total Fat: 20g
- Saturated Fat: 12g
- Carbohydrates: 22g
- Protein: 8g
- Fiber: 2g
- Sugar: 2g
- Salt: 380mg

Baked Camembert Wreath

Prep Time: 10 minutes   **Cook Time:** 20 minutes   **Servings:** 6-8

Ingredients

- 1 whole Camembert cheese (around 250g)
- 1 sheet of puff pastry
- 1 egg (beaten, for egg wash)
- 2 tbsp honey
- 1 tbsp fresh rosemary, chopped
- 1 tbsp olive oil
- Salt and pepper, to taste
- 1 small handful of walnuts (optional)
- Fresh fruit or chutney, for serving (optional)

Instructions

1. Preheat the oven to 200ºC (180ºC fan) or 400ºF. Unwrap the Camembert and place it in the centre of the puff pastry sheet. Using a sharp knife, make small cuts around the edge of the cheese, being careful not to cut through it completely. Drizzle honey over the top of the cheese and sprinkle with chopped rosemary, salt, and pepper.

2. Wrap the puff pastry around the cheese, folding the edges over to form a wreath shape. If you have excess pastry, you can twist it into a braid or simple pattern to decorate the wreath. Brush the pastry with the beaten egg to give it a golden finish when baked.

3. Place the wreath onto a baking sheet lined with parchment paper and bake in the preheated oven for 15-20 minutes, or until the pastry is golden brown and puffed up. Once baked, remove from the oven and drizzle with extra honey. Optionally, sprinkle with walnuts for added texture and serve with fresh fruit or chutney on the side.

Nutritional Information (per serving)

- Calories: 300 kcal
- Total Fat: 20g
- Saturated Fat: 8g
- Carbohydrates: 21g
- Protein: 7g
- Fiber: 1g
- Sugar: 8g
- Salt: 400mg

Pizza Puff Pinwheels

Prep Time: 15 minutes   **Cook Time:** 20 minutes   **Servings:** 4

Ingredients

- **1 sheet of puff pastry (250g)**
- **100g pizza sauce or tomato passata**
- **100g grated mozzarella cheese**
- **50g pepperoni slices (optional)**
- **1 tsp dried oregano**
- **1 egg (for egg wash)**
- **Olive oil (for brushing)**
- **Salt and pepper, to taste**

Instructions

1. Start by preheating your oven to 200ºC (180ºC fan) or 400ºF. Roll out the puff pastry sheet onto a lightly floured surface. Spread the pizza sauce evenly over the surface of the pastry, leaving a small border around the edges. Sprinkle the grated mozzarella cheese over the sauce, followed by the pepperoni slices (if using). Season with a pinch of dried oregano, salt, and pepper.

2. Carefully roll up the puff pastry from one side, creating a tight log. Slice the rolled pastry into about 8-10 equal pieces. Place the pinwheels onto a baking tray lined with parchment paper. Whisk the egg and brush it over the top of each pinwheel to give them a golden finish when baked.

3. Bake the pinwheels in the preheated oven for about 15-20 minutes or until they are puffed up and golden brown. Remove them from the oven and let them cool slightly before serving.

Nutritional Information (per serving)

- Calories: 230 kcal
- Total Fat: 16g
- Saturated Fat: 7g
- Carbohydrates: 18g
- Protein: 7g
- Fiber: 1g
- Sugar: 1g
- Salt: 450mg

Slider Cheeseburger Tray

Prep Time: 15 minutes   **Cook Time:** 20 minutes   **Servings:** 6

Ingredients

- **500g lean ground beef**
- **1 small onion, finely chopped**
- **1 tsp garlic powder**
- **1 tsp paprika**
- **Salt and pepper, to taste**
- **6 small burger buns, split in half**
- **6 slices of cheddar cheese**
- **2 tbsp tomato ketchup**
- **2 tbsp mustard**
- **2 tbsp mayonnaise**
- **1 tbsp melted butter**
- **Pickles, for garnish (optional)**
- **Fresh lettuce leaves, for serving**

Instructions

1. Preheat your oven to 180°C (350°F) and line a baking tray with parchment paper. In a large bowl, combine the ground beef, finely chopped onion, garlic powder, paprika, salt, and pepper. Mix together until evenly combined. Press the beef mixture into the baking tray to form an even layer, making sure the beef is spread out to the edges of the tray.
2. Bake in the preheated oven for 15-18 minutes, or until the beef is fully cooked through. Remove from the oven and place the bun halves on top of the beef layer, cut-side up. Add a slice of cheddar cheese on top of each bun half, and return the tray to the oven for another 3-4 minutes, or until the cheese has melted and the buns are lightly toasted.
3. Meanwhile, mix together the ketchup, mustard, and mayonnaise in a small bowl. Once the cheese has melted and the buns are golden, remove the tray from the oven. Spread a generous amount of the sauce mixture on the inside of each top bun, then place the bun tops onto the slider bases. If you like, garnish with pickles and serve with fresh lettuce leaves on the side.

Nutritional Information (per serving)

- Calories: 370 kcal
- Total Fat: 20g
- Saturated Fat: 8g

- Carbohydrates: 29g
- Protein: 22g
- Fiber: 1g
- Sugar: 4g
- Salt: 700mg

TikTok Charcuterie Board Art

Prep Time: 15 minutes   **Cook Time:** 0 minutes   **Servings:** 4-6

Ingredients

- **150g assorted cured meats (salami, prosciutto, chorizo)**
- **100g soft cheese (Brie or Camembert)**
- **100g hard cheese (Cheddar or Manchego)**
- **100g grapes, halved**
- **1 small jar of mixed olives**
- **2-3 tablespoons of honey or fruit preserves**
- **1 cup of dried fruits (apricots, figs, or raisins)**
- **1 small baguette or crackers**
- **Fresh herbs for garnish (rosemary, thyme)**

Instructions

1. To create the perfect charcuterie board, begin by selecting a large, flat surface or serving board. Arrange the assorted cured meats in a fan shape or rolled into small bundles, placing them evenly across the board. Next, cut the soft cheese into wedges and place them in one corner of the board, followed by chunks of hard cheese in another area.
2. Scatter the halved grapes around the cheeses, adding vibrant pops of colour. Fill in the gaps with small bowls of mixed olives and a jar of honey or fruit preserves for sweetness.
3. Lay out the dried fruits in a decorative pattern, creating a contrast with the savoury elements. For a finishing touch, slice the baguette into thin pieces or serve with crackers placed neatly along one side of the board.
4. Add a few sprigs of fresh rosemary or thyme to enhance the aesthetic. Serve immediately with a variety of drinks like wine or sparkling water.

Nutritional Information (per serving)

- Calories: 400 kcal
- Total Fat: 30g
- Saturated Fat: 10g
- Carbohydrates: 30g
- Protein: 12g
- Fiber: 5g
- Sugar: 15g
- Salt: 600mg

Korean BBQ Lettuce Wraps

Prep Time: 15 minutes   **Cook Time:** 10 minutes   **Servings:** 4

Ingredients

- **500g minced beef or pork (or a mix of both)**
- **1 tablespoon sesame oil**
- **3 cloves garlic, minced**
- **1 small onion, finely chopped**
- **2 tablespoons soy sauce**
- **1 tablespoon gochujang**
- **(Korean chili paste)**
- **1 tablespoon honey or brown sugar**
- **1 tablespoon rice vinegar**
- **1 tablespoon toasted sesame seeds**
- **1 teaspoon grated ginger**
- **12 large lettuce leaves (butter**
- **lettuce or iceberg work well)**
- **1 small cucumber, julienned**
- **1 carrot, julienned**
- **Fresh coriander (optional)**
- **1 tablespoon vegetable oil for cooking**

Instructions

1. In a large pan, heat the vegetable oil over medium heat. Add the minced meat and cook until browned, breaking it up as it cooks, about 5-7 minutes. Drain excess fat if necessary.

2. Add sesame oil to the pan with the minced garlic, onion, and ginger. Sauté for 2-3 minutes until the onion softens and the garlic becomes fragrant. Stir in the soy sauce, gochujang, honey, and rice vinegar. Let it simmer for 2-3 minutes until the sauce thickens slightly and the flavours meld.

3. Remove the pan from the heat and stir in the sesame seeds. Taste and adjust seasoning if necessary, adding more soy sauce, honey, or gochujang to suit your preferences.

4. To assemble, carefully wash and dry the lettuce leaves. Place a spoonful of the meat mixture in the centre of each lettuce leaf. Top with a few pieces of julienned cucumber and carrot, and garnish with fresh coriander if desired.

5. Serve the wraps immediately, folding the lettuce around the filling like a taco.

Nutritional Information (per serving)

- Calories: 300 kcal
- Total Fat: 20g
- Saturated Fat: 4g
- Carbohydrates: 14g
- Protein: 20g
- Fiber: 3g
- Sugar: 6g
- Salt: 700mg

Stuffed Peppers with Chorizo

Prep Time: 15 minutes   **Cook Time:** 30 minutes   **Servings:** 4

Ingredients

- **4 large bell peppers (red, yellow, or green)**
- **200g chorizo sausage, casing removed and crumbled**
- **1 small onion, finely chopped**
- **2 cloves garlic, minced**
- **1 cup cooked rice (white or brown)**
- **1 tin (400g) chopped tomatoes**
- **1 teaspoon smoked paprika**
- **1/2 teaspoon dried oregano**
- **1/2 cup grated cheddar cheese**
- **Salt and pepper, to taste**
- **Olive oil for cooking**
- **Fresh parsley, chopped (for garnish)**

Instructions

1. Preheat Oven and Prepare Peppers: Preheat the oven to 180°C (160°C fan) or 350°F. Cut the tops off the bell peppers and remove the seeds and membranes. Set the peppers aside.
2. Cook Chorizo: In a large frying pan, heat a little olive oil over medium heat. Add the crumbled chorizo and cook for about 5-6 minutes until it starts to crisp up and release its oil. Remove the chorizo from the pan and set aside.
3. Sauté Onion and Garlic: In the same pan, add the chopped onion and cook for about 3 minutes until softened. Add the minced garlic and cook for another 30 seconds, until fragrant.
4. Prepare Stuffing: Add the cooked rice to the pan with the onions and garlic. Stir in the chopped tomatoes, smoked paprika, and oregano. Season with salt and pepper to taste. Add the cooked chorizo back into the pan and mix everything together.
5. Stuff the Peppers: Spoon the chorizo and rice mixture into the prepared bell peppers, packing the filling tightly. Place the stuffed peppers in a baking dish.
6. Bake: Cover the dish with aluminium foil and bake in the preheated oven for 20 minutes. After 20 minutes, remove the foil, sprinkle the grated cheddar cheese over the stuffed peppers, and return them to the oven for an additional 10 minutes, or until the cheese is melted and bubbly.
7. Serve: Garnish with chopped fresh parsley and serve warm.

Nutritional Information (per serving)

- Calories: 380 kcal
- Total Fat: 24g
- Saturated Fat: 9g
- Carbohydrates: 20g
- Protein: 20g
- Fiber: 4g
- Sugar: 7g
- Salt: 900mg

Mini Pitta Pizza Bites

Prep Time: 10 minutes   **Cook Time:** 10 minutes   **Servings:** 4

Ingredients

- **4 small wholemeal pittas**
- **100g tomato passata**
- **1 tsp dried oregano**
- **1 tsp garlic powder**
- **150g mozzarella cheese, grated**
- **50g pepperoni slices (or preferred topping)**
- **Fresh basil leaves (optional)**
- **Salt and pepper, to taste**
- **Olive oil for drizzling**

Instructions

1. To make the sauce, combine the tomato passata, oregano, garlic powder, salt, and pepper in a bowl, and mix well. Cut each pitta in half to create 8 mini bases.
2. Place them on a baking tray lined with parchment paper. Spread a thin layer of the tomato sauce onto each pitta half. Sprinkle grated mozzarella evenly on top of each base.
3. Add your chosen toppings, such as pepperoni slices, or any other preferred vegetables. Drizzle with a little olive oil and season with salt and pepper. Preheat your oven to 200°C (180°C fan) or 400°F.
4. Bake the pitta pizzas in the oven for 8-10 minutes, or until the cheese is melted and golden, and the pittas are crispy. Once done, remove from the oven and top with fresh basil leaves if desired. Slice and serve hot.

Nutritional Information (per serving)

- Calories: 310 kcal
- Total Fat: 16g
- Saturated Fat: 7g
- Carbohydrates: 29g
- Protein: 14g
- Fiber: 5g
- Sugar: 3g
- Salt: 600mg

Sticky Honey Garlic Meatballs

Prep Time: 15 minutes   **Cook Time:** 20 minutes   **Servings:** 4

Ingredients

- **500g minced pork or beef**
- **1 small onion, finely chopped**
- **2 cloves garlic, minced**
- **1 large egg**
- **50g breadcrumbs**
- **1 tbsp fresh parsley, chopped**
- **2 tbsp olive oil**
- **Salt and pepper, to taste**
- **3 tbsp honey**
- **3 tbsp soy sauce**
- **2 tbsp rice vinegar**
- **1 tbsp sesame oil**

- **1 tsp grated ginger (optional)**
- **1 tsp sesame seeds (optional)**

Instructions

1. To make the meatballs, combine the minced pork or beef with the chopped onion, minced garlic, egg, breadcrumbs, chopped parsley, and salt and pepper in a large bowl. Mix everything together until well combined, then form the mixture into small meatballs, about the size of a walnut.

2. Heat the olive oil in a large frying pan over medium heat. Add the meatballs to the pan and cook for 10-12 minutes, turning occasionally, until golden brown and cooked through. Once cooked, remove the meatballs from the pan and set aside.

3. In the same pan, combine the honey, soy sauce, rice vinegar, sesame oil, and grated ginger (if using). Bring to a simmer, stirring frequently, until the sauce thickens slightly, about 3-4 minutes.

4. Return the meatballs to the pan and toss them in the sticky sauce until fully coated. Let them simmer in the sauce for another 2-3 minutes to absorb the flavours.

5. Serve the sticky honey garlic meatballs hot, garnished with sesame seeds and extra parsley if desired.

Nutritional Information (per serving)

- Calories: 320 kcal
- Total Fat: 18g
- Saturated Fat: 4g
- Carbohydrates: 20g
- Protein: 21g
- Fiber: 1g
- Sugar: 15g
- Salt: 700mg

TikTok Cooking Challenges

TikTok has revolutionised the way we approach cooking, and one of the most exciting aspects of the platform is the rise of cooking challenges. These challenges push your culinary creativity to new heights while keeping things fun, fast, and often, incredibly simple! Whether you're a beginner or an experienced cook, you'll love trying out these TikTok cooking challenges, which bring the thrill of experimentation right into your kitchen. Here are three of the most popular TikTok cooking trends that you can easily recreate and enjoy!

The 5-Minute Recipe Challenge

In this fast-paced challenge, the goal is simple: create a delicious dish in just five minutes! This challenge encourages quick thinking, minimal prep time, and creativity with ingredients you already have in your kitchen. The beauty of the 5-minute recipe challenge is that it's all about speed without compromising on taste. Whether you're in a rush or just craving a quick bite, this challenge is the perfect way to test your cooking skills under pressure.

Tips for Success:
- Keep your ingredients prepped and ready to go—time is of the essence!
- Choose simple ingredients that don't require much cooking, like avocado, eggs, or bread.
- Use a timer to keep yourself on track, and challenge yourself to improve your time with each recipe!

Popular 5-Minute Recipe Ideas:
- Avocado toast with an egg
- Quick veggie stir-fry
- Microwave mug cakes
- Instant smoothie bowls

No-Recipe Cooking Trend

The no-recipe cooking trend has taken TikTok by storm, encouraging people to cook without following any strict guidelines. It's all about using what you have on hand, making it up as you go, and experimenting with flavours and textures. This challenge is perfect for the adventurous home cook who enjoys freedom in the kitchen and wants to push their creativity.

How It Works:
- Start by picking a basic ingredient or two—such as pasta, chicken, or veggies.
- Add seasonings, herbs, and spices based on your instincts and taste.
- Try out different combinations of flavours, cooking methods, and textures.
- Don't be afraid to try something new—whether it's sweet, savoury, or spicy!

Tips for Success:

- Trust your intuition! If you think a certain ingredient or spice will work well, go for it.
- Keep it simple. Sometimes, the best dishes are made with the fewest ingredients.
- If you're unsure, take inspiration from what others have done on TikTok and make it your own!

Popular No-Recipe Cooking Ideas:

- One-pan pasta dishes
- Stir-fried vegetables with any sauce you like
- Skillet eggs with various toppings
- Toast with anything from cream cheese to fruit

3-Ingredient Masterpieces

The 3-Ingredient Masterpieces challenge is exactly what it sounds like—creating incredible dishes with only three ingredients! This challenge is all about making the most of a small number of ingredients while maximising flavour. It encourages simplicity and teaches you how to get creative with the basics. You'll be surprised at how delicious and impressive a dish can be with so few ingredients.

How It Works:

- Choose your three main ingredients, which should ideally complement each other.
- Use these ingredients to create a dish—whether it's a snack, dessert, or meal.
- Focus on balancing flavours and textures, and get creative with combinations!

Tips for Success:

- Think about textures and flavours that will work well together, such as sweet, salty, and sour.
- Use pantry staples as your base—things like pasta, rice, eggs, and canned vegetables are perfect.
- Keep an eye on TikTok for inspiration and make adjustments based on your preferences.

Popular 3-Ingredient Masterpieces:

- Peanut butter cookies (peanut butter, sugar, and egg)
- 3-ingredient pizza dough
- 3-ingredient pancakes
- Sweet potato fries (sweet potatoes, olive oil, and seasoning)

TikTok cooking challenges are a fantastic way to have fun in the kitchen and experiment with new ideas, all while honing your cooking skills. Whether you're racing against the clock with the 5-minute recipe challenge, using your intuition with the no-recipe trend, or creating stunning dishes with just three ingredients, these challenges will inspire you to think outside the recipe box and discover new flavours and techniques. Ready to take on the challenge? Let your creativity run wild and enjoy the process!

Conclusion

Embrace Your Inner TikTok Chef

By now, you've explored the vibrant, creative, and ever-evolving world of TikTok cooking. From viral trends to time-saving hacks, from quick-and-easy recipes to gourmet-inspired creations, this cookbook has introduced you to the magic of social media-driven culinary exploration. But this journey is just the beginning.

Embracing your inner TikTok chef means more than just following trends; it's about unleashing your creativity, experimenting with flavors, and making every meal an experience. TikTok has revolutionized how we cook, making the kitchen a playground where food becomes an expression of individuality and joy. Whether you're a seasoned home cook or a kitchen newbie, you now have the tools, inspiration, and confidence to craft delicious meals with ease and flair.

The beauty of TikTok cooking lies in its accessibility and community. Cooking no longer has to feel like a chore—it's an interactive experience, a form of self-expression, and even a way to connect with millions of like-minded food lovers. By embracing this digital culinary revolution, you are joining a movement that celebrates innovation, culture, and most importantly, flavor.

So, what's next? Keep experimenting. Keep sharing. Keep challenging yourself. Take these recipes as a foundation and add your personal twist. Make your own food hacks, remix trending recipes, and inspire others with your creations. Who knows? Your next dish might just go viral!

The kitchen is now your stage, and the world is watching. So grab your ingredients, hit record, and let your culinary journey unfold—one delicious, TikTok-worthy bite at a time.

Sharing Your Creations Online

One of the most exciting parts of TikTok cooking is the ability to share your culinary masterpieces with the world. Whether you're showing off a beautifully plated dish, demonstrating a clever cooking hack, or putting your own twist on a viral recipe, social media gives you the perfect platform to inspire others.

When sharing your creations online, consider using trending hashtags to reach a wider audience. Engage with fellow food creators by commenting on their posts, participating in challenges, and collaborating on duets. The more you interact, the more your content will be discovered by food lovers across the globe.

Quality matters, too! Good lighting, clear step-by-step demonstrations, and a touch of personality can make your videos stand out. Don't be afraid to experiment with different styles—whether it's quick recipe demos, ASMR cooking, or behind-the-scenes clips, your unique approach is what makes your content special.

Most importantly, have fun! TikTok cooking is all about creativity, community, and the joy of making delicious food. So, keep sharing, keep learning, and keep cooking—you never know when your next recipe will become the internet's new favorite trend!

Bonus Tips

By now, you've explored the vibrant, creative, and ever-evolving world of TikTok cooking. From viral trends to time-saving hacks, from quick-and-easy recipes to gourmet-inspired creations, this cookbook has introduced you to the magic of social media-driven culinary exploration. But this journey is just the beginning.

Embracing your inner TikTok chef means more than just following trends; it's about unleashing your creativity, experimenting with flavors, and making every meal an experience. TikTok has revolutionized how we cook, making the kitchen a playground where food becomes an expression of individuality and joy. Whether you're a seasoned home cook or a kitchen newbie, you now have the tools, inspiration, and confidence to craft delicious meals with ease and flair.

Sharing Your Creations Online

One of the most exciting parts of TikTok cooking is the ability to share your culinary masterpieces with the world. Whether you're showing off a beautifully plated dish, demonstrating a clever cooking hack, or putting your own twist on a viral recipe, social media gives you the perfect platform to inspire others.

When sharing your creations online, consider using trending hashtags to reach a wider audience. Engage with fellow food creators by commenting on their posts, participating in challenges, and collaborating on duets. The more you interact, the more your content will be discovered by food lovers across the globe.

Quality matters, too! Good lighting, clear step-by-step demonstrations, and a touch of personality can make your videos stand out. Don't be afraid to experiment with different styles—whether it's quick recipe demos, ASMR cooking, or behind-the-scenes clips, your unique approach is what makes your content special.

Most importantly, have fun! TikTok cooking is all about creativity, community, and the joy of making delicious food. So, keep sharing, keep learning, and keep cooking—you never know when your next recipe will become the internet's new favorite trend!

1. Preheat your oven to 200°C (180°C fan) or 400°F. Line a baking tray with parchment paper.
2. Grate the cauliflower or pulse it in a food processor until it resembles rice. Place it in a clean kitchen towel or cheesecloth and squeeze out as much moisture as possible.
3. In a large bowl, combine the cauliflower with mozzarella, Parmesan, egg, oregano, garlic powder, onion powder, and season with salt and pepper. Mix everything together until a dough-like consistency forms.
4. Take small spoonfuls of the mixture and shape them into bite-sized discs. Place them on the prepared baking tray, ensuring they are evenly spaced.
5. Bake for 15-20 minutes, or until the cauliflower bites are golden and crispy on the edges.
6. Once out of the oven, spread a small spoonful of tomato sauce on each cauliflower bite. Top with mini pepperoni (if using) and return to the oven for an additional 5 minutes, until the cheese is melted.
7. Remove from the oven and garnish with fresh basil leaves, if desired. Serve warm.

Nutritional Information (per serving)

- Calories: 140 kcal
- Total Fat: 9g
- Saturated Fat: 4g
- Carbohydrates: 6g
- Protein: 12g
- Fiber: 3g
- Sugar: 2g
- Salt: 350mg

Sweet Potato Toast Trio

Prep Time: 10 minutes   **Cook Time:** 15 minutes   **Servings:** 2

Ingredients

- 1 large sweet potato
- 1 tablespoon olive oil
- Salt and pepper, to taste

Topping 1: Avocado & Cherry Tomato

- 1 ripe avocado, mashed
- 6 cherry tomatoes, halved

Instructions

- A sprinkle of chilli flakes

Topping 2: Peanut Butter & Banana

- 2 tablespoons natural peanut butter
- 1 small banana, sliced
- A drizzle of honey

Topping 3: Greek Yoghurt & Berries

- 3 tablespoons plain Greek yoghurt
- A handful of mixed berries (blueberries, raspberries, or strawberries)
- A sprinkle of granola

- 2 medium sweet potatoes, thinly sliced
- 2 medium carrots, thinly sliced
- 1 courgette (zucchini), thinly sliced
- 1 tablespoon olive oil
- 1 teaspoon paprika
- 1 teaspoon garlic powder
- 1/2 teaspoon sea salt
- Freshly ground black pepper, to taste

Instructions

1. Preheat your oven to 180°C (160°C fan) or 350°F. Line a baking tray with parchment paper. In a large bowl, toss the thinly sliced sweet potatoes, carrots, and courgette with olive oil until evenly coated.
2. Sprinkle over the paprika, garlic powder, sea salt, and freshly ground black pepper. Toss everything together to ensure the vegetables are well-seasoned.
3. Spread the vegetables out in a single layer on the prepared baking tray. Be sure not to overcrowd them, as this will help them crisp up better. Bake in the preheated oven for 20-25 minutes, flipping the crisps halfway through.
4. The veggies should be golden and crispy when done. Remove from the oven and let them cool for a few minutes before serving.

Nutritional Information (per serving)

- Calories: 130 kcal
- Total Fat: 6g
- Saturated Fat: 0.5g
- Carbohydrates: 20g
- Protein: 2g
- Fiber: 5g
- Sugar: 5g
- Salt: 350mg

Low-Cal Cauliflower Pizza Bites

Prep Time: 15 minutes   **Cook Time:** 20 minutes   **Servings:** 4

Ingredients

- 1 medium cauliflower, grated or processed into rice-sized pieces
- 100g mozzarella cheese, grated
- 50g Parmesan cheese, grated
- 1 large egg
- 1 tsp dried oregano
- 1/2 tsp garlic powder
- 1/2 tsp onion powder
- Salt and pepper, to taste
- 2 tbsp tomato sauce (for topping)
- 1/4 cup mini pepperoni (optional)
- Fresh basil leaves, for garnish (optional)

Instructions

Bonus Tips for Mastering TikTok Cooking

Want to take your TikTok cooking game to the next level? Here are some expert tips to help you make the most out of your culinary journey:

- **Master the Basics** – Before diving into advanced techniques, ensure you have a solid foundation. Learn essential knife skills, cooking methods, and ingredient pairings to elevate your dishes effortlessly.
- **Plan Your Content** – Prepping in advance can make filming smoother. Outline your recipe steps, gather ingredients, and set up your workspace before hitting record.
- **Use High-Quality Ingredients** – Fresh, high-quality ingredients make a big difference in taste and presentation. They also photograph and film better, making your content more visually appealing.
- **Optimize for Engagement** – Keep your videos short, engaging, and straight to the point. The first few seconds matter the most, so start with an exciting hook to capture viewers' attention.
- **Leverage Trends Wisely** – While following food trends can boost your reach, don't be afraid to add your unique spin. Creative variations on popular recipes can make your content stand out.
- **Experiment with Editing** – Use TikTok's built-in tools to enhance your videos. Speed up steps, add captions, incorporate fun transitions, and include background music to create an engaging experience.
- **Engage with Your Audience** – Reply to comments, ask for feedback, and encourage viewers to try your recipes. Building a community around your content can lead to more shares and followers.
- **Work on Your Presentation** – A well-plated dish can make all the difference. Experiment with plating techniques, colorful ingredients, and aesthetically pleasing backgrounds.
- **Tell a Story** – People love relatable content. Share your personal experience with the dish, its cultural background, or why it's special to you. Storytelling adds depth to your videos.
- **Be Consistent** – Posting regularly helps keep your audience engaged. Whether it's once a day or a few times a week, find a schedule that works for you and stick with it.

The world of TikTok cooking is full of endless possibilities. With these tips in mind, you're ready to create, share, and inspire others with your delicious innovations. So grab your phone, start filming, and let your kitchen creativity shine!

Essential TikTok Hashtags for Foodies

Hashtags are a powerful tool to increase the visibility of your food content on TikTok. Using the right hashtags can help you reach food lovers, fellow creators, and potential followers. Here are some essential hashtags to include in your posts:

General Food Hashtags
#FoodTok
#TikTokEats
#Foodie
#HomeCooking
#Yum

Aesthetic Hashtags
#FoodPhotography
#FoodArt
#PlatingGoals
#InstaFood
#Gourmet

Trending & Viral Food Hashtags
#FoodTrend
#ViralRecipe
#TrendingFood
#MustTry
#FoodHack

Diet & Lifestyle Hashtags
#KetoFood
#VeganEats
#GlutenFree
#HighProtein
#LowCarb

Recipe-Specific Hashtags
#EasyRecipe
#QuickMeals
#HealthyEating
#ComfortFood
#DessertLover

Cultural & Cuisine-Based Hashtags
#ItalianFood
#MexicanFood
#AsianCuisine
#SoulFood
#StreetFood

Thank You

for joining us on this flavorful journey through the world of **TikTok cooking!** We hope this cookbook has inspired you to try new recipes, experiment with flavors, and have fun in the kitchen. Your support means the world to us, and we'd love to hear about your experience!

If you enjoyed this cookbook, we'd greatly appreciate it if you could leave a review. Your feedback helps us improve and create even better content in the future. Plus, your review might just help another aspiring TikTok chef discover their next favorite recipe.

Happy cooking, and don't forget to share your delicious creations with the world!

Printed in Dunstable, United Kingdom